SCOTLAND
N.
Hadrian's Wall
ENGLAND
LONDON
CORNWALL
G.W.

Come Away to England

Sequel to
Dorset Forever
and
Return to Wessex

Dedicated to my students
With the hope that . . .
    Their souls to God will ever belong,
    Their hands be strong in duty,
    Ears be tuned to sweetest song,
    And their eyes be filled with beauty.

Gwen Woodruff

Come Away to England

Photographs by Dick Woodruff
Sketches, maps and designs
by Gwen Woodruff

Birmingham, Alabama
1988

Books by the same author:
Return to Wessex   *(published 1983)*
Dorset Forever   *(published 1981)*

First Edition

Library of Congress Catalog Card Number 88-50955

Color separations and B & W negatives
—Precision Color Inc., Birmingham, AL.
Font—Goudy Oldstyle, 12.5 Pt.

Printed in the United States of America
by Commercial Printing Co.
Birmingham, Alabama 35202

ISBN 0-9616165-2-0

CONTENTS

Published by Woodruff Publishing Co.
4153 Kennesaw Drive
Birmingham, Alabama 35213
U.S.A.
1988

I read once the lines of H.V. Morton: "I would go home in search of England, I would go through the lanes of England and the little thatched villages of England, and I would lean over English bridges and lie on English grass watching an English sky."

So I went. I followed my mood . . . . into hamlets that books had not pre-empted, village lanes untrod by tourist's feet; I talked with lords and ladies . . . . tramps and animals . . . . lay on the verdant sward and watched the winds push masses of fluffy clouds into amazing shapes. This was my adventure.

Introduction

The Peace of Westphalia, the Utrecht Settlement, the Edict of Nantes, the Holy League, ... and on and on rants the historian. His is the job of recorder of actual occurrences as pertaining to the effect on world framework. And the archaeologist is busy with his scientific analyzing of remains of past civilizations — he thinks more of his crumbling shards than of a Cellini sculpturing. Then there's the biologist and his concern with living organisms. But here is the lowly romanticist who lingers after sunset caressing a fifteenth century gatepost where some configuration had been carved long ago bearing more significance to her than all the boundary lines, Rosetta Stones, Pragmatic Sanctions, Albigensian Crusades, or Manichean heretics. And now we have Starwars practically invading us! So please come away with me . . . . away from this frenzied suspension between nuclear disaster or world starvation.

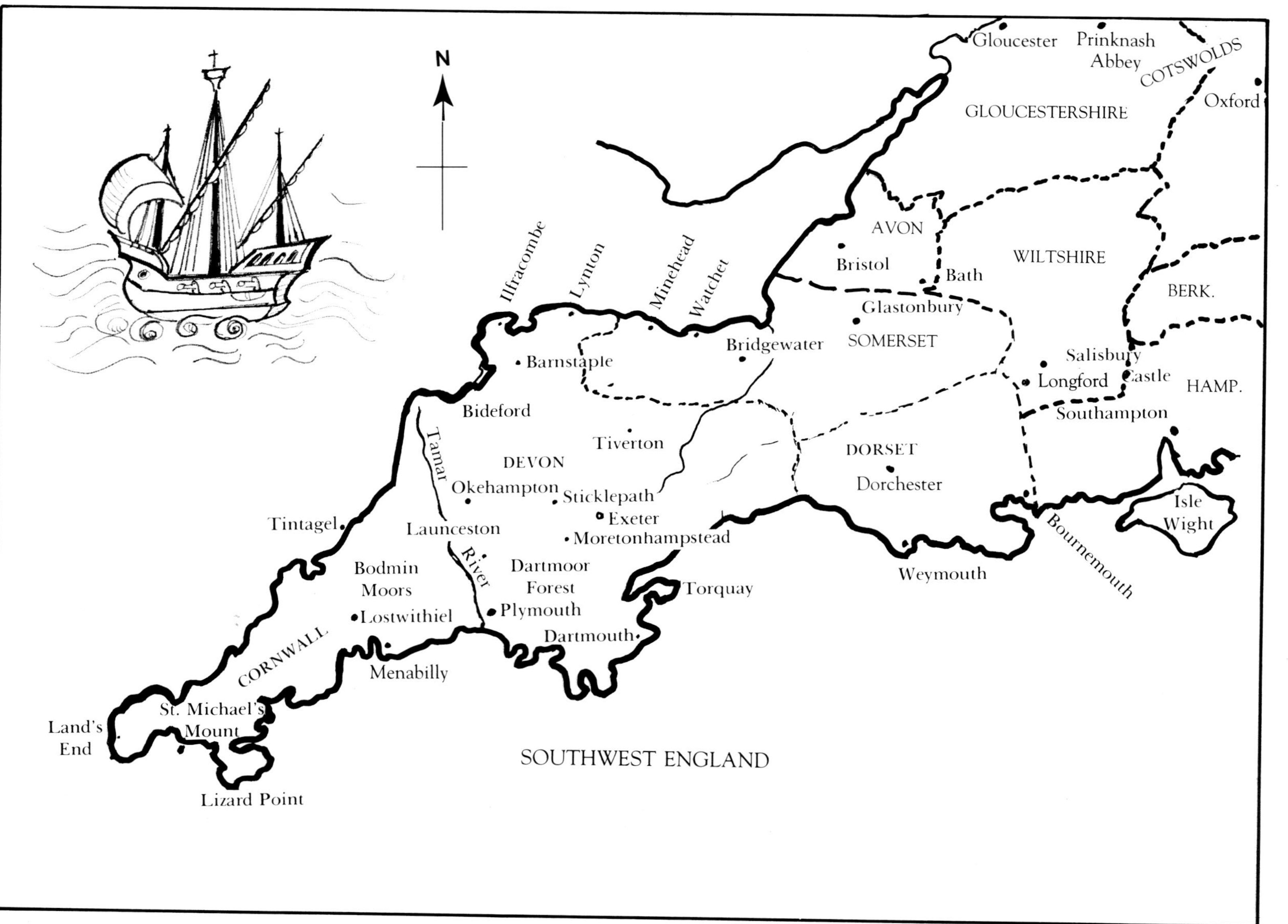

Gloucester
Prinknash Abbey
COTSWOLDS
Oxford
GLOUCESTERSHIRE
AVON
Bristol
Bath
WILTSHIRE
BERK.
Glastonbury
SOMERSET
Salisbury
Longford Castle
HAMP.
Southampton
Bridgewater
Ilfracombe
Lynton
Minehead
Watchet
Barnstaple
Bideford
Tiverton
DEVON
DORSET
Dorchester
Okehampton
Sticklepath
Exeter
Moretonhampstead
Tintagel
Launceston
Tamar
River
Bodmin Moors
Dartmoor Forest
Plymouth
Torquay
Weymouth
Bournemouth
Isle Wight
Lostwithiel
Dartmouth
CORNWALL
Menabilly
St. Michael's Mount
Land's End
Lizard Point
N
SOUTHWEST ENGLAND

In Avonshire

Late afternoon shadows were engulfing the grassy meadows — tiny slivers of red-gold clung to the western hillside. And here came Brother Paul with his arms full of bedding and towels. We must make up our own rooms . . . . "if you don't mind," his eyes apologized, "the doors will be locked at nine o'clock." We followed his padded slippers into the huge abbey kitchen and were shown where the breakfast fixings were kept. There were eggs, fresh butter, milk, honey, cornflakes, bread — everything for an Englishman's appetite.

I touched his sleeve, "I must know about the carved flower on the priory gate."

But First . . .

This was in 1983. Something new had happened in England . . . . where nothing *ever* changed. She had a new county. Avonshire had been carved out of bits of surrounding Somerset, Wiltshire and Gloucester. Bristol was its capital. This was our destination because the Isambard Kingdom Brunel Sesquicentennial was being held there. In 1831 the Clifton Suspension Bridge was started by Brunel and was an ambitious project indeed. Serving as one of the

Prinknash Abbey is a jewel of Southwestern England in Avonshire. It was built in King Alfred the Great's ninth century.

A different view of Prinknash. It was used as a hunting lodge by Henry VIII; he often brought Catherine of Aragon with him.

directors of the American Society of Civil Engineers, my husband was invited to attend the affair as the guest of the Bristol Mayor. This was why we were in the area of Gloucester, which would attract us to the Abbey. Arriving several days early for the gala event we wandered over the hillside in the direction of the great Cathedral of Gloucester. Nothing seemed different since our last visit of several years ago; inside the colossal walls Edward II, the poor maligned son of Edward I, who was murdered (most likely by his queen Isabella and her lover Roger Mortimer at Berkeley Castle) slept on in his gorgeous canopied tomb. Edward III, his son, erected it for him in 1330, while his mother was held prisoner at Castle Rising. There is nothing in this world in stonework to equal the beauty of this sarcophagus — not even the white and black touchstone monument of Henry VII in Westminster Abbey carved by Torregiani (c. 1512) can compare with the delicate frozen lace here. (Incidentally, Torregiani of Florence was the impetuous young Italian who broke Michelangelo's nose.)

2

Let's leave the dead in peace and resume our journey to the 'Monastery of the Cotswolds'. Suddenly a teasing jingle started in my head . . . . what on earth *did* 'Doctor Foster' go to Gloucester for?

Doctor Foster went to Gloucester
In a shower of rain
He stepped in a puddle right up to his middle
And never went there again.

Avonshire was recently carved from bits of surrounding Somerset, Wilts, and Gloucester. Bristol is its capital. Shown here is the oldest pub in the city.

Then the nursery rhyme came back to me. Well, at least there's no rain puddling today. It was simply lovely — and as we stepped out of the cathedral a big yellow cat slunk in beside me and rubbed my leg. Wow! was that 'Simpkin' . . . . he shouldn't be here! Wasn't he in Beatrix Potter's story? Think I'm getting them all mixed up with the "Tailor of Gloucester."

4

We will drive southward on the B4703 road to Upton
Leonard. Signs should be appearing, as the tremendous
grounds of the Abbey Park are only five miles from the
cathedral. You can expect something — the likes of which
you will never again experience. In the glorious fields of the
Cotswold countryside is nestled a jewel of the ninth century — not a partial ruin from King Alfred's day but a glowing, growing miracle that has only recently reached its
zenith by the ingenuity of the twentieth century Benedictine Monks.

In ancient documents Prinknash — which *is* that
jewel — was spelled many ways: Prinkmarsh, Prinknesse,
Prinkendge, Prignes, but now the phonetic confusion has
resolved itself and it will be Prinknash (pronounced
Prinage) from now on. First we were confronted with a large
golden building of contemporary style; this was where we
were to inquire about a friend's brother who was 'head'
monk. Finding him away in hospital with appendicitis, we
identified ourselves and expressed our desire to deliver

5

felicitations from his sister who had moved to Alabama. We were invited to stay the night in the guest house .... and that is what started my unforgetable romance with the place.

Back to the rosette on the gateway where we had entered. I knew that Henry VIII and Catherine of Aragon spent some time here, making it his hunting lodge .... and I will talk more about that later. Catherine, the daughter of the Catholic Queen of Spain, had married her English brother-in-law after her husband (Prince Arthur) died and left her .... and she such a young bride. Queen Isabella had given the fifteen year old Catherine an exquisite jewelled Pomegranate upon her departure from Spain. This royal symbol now rests in the British Museum of London. A donor (thought to be an American) presented the exotic fifteenth century ornament to the museum. Strong testimony gives credence to its genuineness. It was brought by Catherine of Aragon to England as part of her dowry. (In recent excavations at Nonsuch Palace, outside of London, it was discovered. This uneclipsed palatial

One of Gloucester's characteristic streets. The adage "as sure as God is in Gloucester" probably refers to the many abbeys and large churches in the area.

wonder in architecture was built by Henry VIII in 1530. We found nothing left when we went searching for remnants of the Palace at Ewell Park, south of London.) My romantic interest was first aroused when I read *The Nonsuch Lure* by Mary Luke. Many visitors to the Alhambra in Granada, Spain, see only a squared complex of buildings rising upon a reddish crag. They purchase their tickets at the magnificent palace of Charles V (never completed), wander along the cool halls of the Moorish palaces, view the Court of the Myrtles, admire the twelve queer, stocky little stone lions — like wooden creatures of a carved Noah's Ark spitting out jets of water into a basin in the Court of the Lions, and look at flower pot after pot of scarlet geraniums. They peer through the arcaded windows at the softened view of Granada beyond — then fumbling in their pockets they search for the car keys, trying to remember where the car was parked. Please stop! The visit doesn't end here; its story only starts at this place. Spain was not an entity until Isabella and Fernando had driven out the last of the Moors: that spineless, vacillating, whimpering oldest son of their Emir in 1466. Isabella had begun her conquest at Burgos to rid Spain of the Moors and Jews. She endured hardships that would have stopped a less indomitable human, and on the sidelines reconnoitered long enough to give birth several different times. Finally, here at Granada in 1492 she would claim her laurels. The disgraced Sultan Boabdil surrendered his lovely Alhambra. In delivering the keys he tried to kiss the conquering Spanish King's hand but was prevented by a stumble. "My Lord, these are the keys to your Alhambra and your City; go, Sire, and possess them." The dispossessed rode away over the mountains crying scalding tears. His mother in bitterness tormented him, "Weep, Son, like a woman for what you could not hold like a man."

When things calmed down — minus the Moors — an intelligent, wide-eyed little girl sat in an Arab kiosk at Alhambra and wrote dutiful letters in Latin to a young prince in Shropshire's Ludlow Castle. Soon she would be leaving her home to join the English King's son for her betrothel. But in the dark future to come (after her second marriage to Arthur's brother) she would long remember the sombre beauty of the land and the exquisite flowers. So in

Henry VIII's first wife came from Spain. She lived in the Alhambra at Granada and admired the twelve stocky little stone lions.

7

8

the waiting hours, while her lord took his pleasure in the hunt, she scratched in the stone her beloved pomegranate blossom at Prinknash.

And I wanted to know more about this floral graffito, but the monks are somewhat inclined to great silence. Brother Paul smiled broadly and gave me a book that I might study the history of the medieval pile of stone and slate. The room we repaired to for our night's rest was the very one King Henry and Catherine had slept in. The daylight was almost gone and I stood by the window and listened to a nest of robins twittering as they settled down for the night. Peace reigned, and I could have been thousands of miles from earth.

Nestling down in my blankets I turned to the story of Prinknash. Only nine o'clock — and locked up without radio or T.V.!

The Early Fifteen Hundreds

Five miles away and four centuries ago Gloucester Abbey's Chapter House had met and they took the oath ordered by the Act of Succession that declared Henry VIII's children by his second wife, Anne Boleyn, to be the lawful heirs to the British Crown. Following this, all the important abbeys were dissolved and turned over to the king's cronies — all the monks and priests scattered abroad. This was 1533. The Benedictine Abbey became a body of secular clerics, and was raised to the rank of Cathedral.

Long before this, though, King Canute (c. 1030) had the 'rule of St. Benedict', who died at Monte Cassino in the sixth century, installed as a code of conduct for a group of devout and holy men that had gathered in Gloucester to give over their lives to poverty, chastity, obedience and hard work. Their good report earned them the award of having the first abbot appointed, but it was not until Edward III's time that they were permitted to hunt deer at nearby Prinknash Park. Almost two hundred years later the hunting manor was given to the abbey as an Abbot's House. They wouldn't enjoy it long though, as by now Henry saw that this was indeed a fair plum to his liking and decreed it his own. After the Tudors, it passed into various hands . . . . the Howells, Ackers, Thomas Dyer Edwards; and each new owner added to and improved the estate. By 1927 the property was becoming a heavy financial burden to the grandson of Dyer Edwards, the 20th Earl of Rothes, so he sacrificed his valuable inheritance to provide a home for a Catholic Benedictine community. The monks left the Isle of Caldey and moved back into the Manor House that had originally been their own. By now their group had grown larger, the old place was too small; they launched out on a plan to build a new monastery. This was completed by 1972. The old Abbey was made into a guest house . . . . and that is where I am now with my head drooping on my chest and eyelids heavy as lead. The book fell to the floor. I was drifting . . . . and all would become oblivion but for the noise of the wild beat of animal hooves in my ears. In my dream I saw King Henry's hunting party returning. Horses would be foaming at their bit . . . . then a sudden thud on the hard earth told me that tired men were dismounting with their heavy trappings. The manor door burst open; voices rose to the upper chamber: "But, my King, I . . . ." interrupted by a roar, "Don't 'but, my King' me . . . . I said it would be tomorrow! We leave at dawn for France to meet Charles and Francis at the Field of Cloth of Gold . . . . and by God's knee, nave, tell the Marquess of Dorset to get that rigged-up contraption from the Courtyard drive. Next he'll be trying to fly to the moon in some gadget he's contrived from his old armour gear." (Heavens, what could I do! I realized it was our car the King was reviling).

"By the Cardinal's toe, I'll have him to the Tower for this . . . the blundering idiot. Here, here, you lazy rogue, make the quarters with more comfort for My Lady Queen Catherine.

"Kate, my sweet Kate, your darling is back."

.... And he catapulted himself into the room that I, four hundred years later, was occupying. One side of the bed suddenly sank downhill, then clunk went a boot .... a shift of the weight, then the second one. And the big hulk stretched out at my side. I rolled over and clung to the far edge — and with a thud I hit the floor.

Dick awoke as I was gaining my perpendicular. "What happened, are you hurt?"

"No, thank heavens I'm safe — what a nightmare. I was afraid we'd have to walk all the way back to Gloucester, what with the Marquess hauling away our 'space ship'."

So much for dreams .... the rest of the night my sleep was undisturbed. The next morning after fixing our breakfast and making a 'donation' to the Abbey we roamed around in the court to find something to substantiate the fabulous symbol of Catherine of Aragon. There at the archway leading into the west entrance I bolted and stood staring; I could just make out a pomegranate on the right of the carving. Now I was convinced of the connections of the abbey with Henry VIII's first wife when I discovered the courtyard pavement laid out in the form of a Catherine Wheel, a device of the royal lady.

Being elated over the finding of this Cotswold treasure we left beautiful Prinknash Abbey. Oh, I forgot .... the monks make a fine pottery that is shipped all over the world.

Then a newspaper article caught my eye .... it said that on a brisk day in late October several people telephoned the police reporting that they'd seen a white minibus cruising through Gloucester's coloured quarter. Silhouetted against the windows were the terrifying shapes of two dozen men in white robes and hoods.

The complaint was taken seriously; a number of suspected racialists were picked up for questioning. One accused man said, "Two officers came to my house and charged me with being a local leader of the clan .... that I had been identified as the driver of the van."

After a month of inquiries the police had nailed down the 'persons of the fiery-cross-followers'. They were Benedictine monks on their way from Prinknash Abbey to a service in Gloucester Cathedral, innocently clad in their ecclesiastical garments.

Even though the monks at Prinknash are familiar and frequent visitors to the city, they do not usually go out in habit and hood. But this time they had changed into clerical garb before leaving the abbey and boarding their minibus.

It was all understandable when it came to light, but "the report we received was genuine and had to be taken seriously", said the police spokesman.

We knew better than to ask directions to Bristol from a native. On a long ago visit to England, landing at Heathrow, we stopped at a petrol station . . . . we suspected the oil level. The attendant asked us to lift the bonnet. "The *What*," I gasped. We inquired about the best way to Uxbridge. "B' Jove now, Love, y'see the ironmonger's place — take the second flyover after the road diversion, pass the lorry park and turn left. At the dual carriageway look out for the roundabout, keep sharp for up-coming signs. Just before the flyover you'll see a lay-by where you can get a good spot of tea." We thanked him profusely for goodness-knows-*what* and made for the nearest store to buy a decent ordnance map of the county.

We will go to Painswick, then to Stroud, swing over on the A4096 to the main A38 to Bristol . . . . as time is of the essence now. We are booked in the Grand Hotel (and grand indeed with sunken tub, hair dryer, clothes presser, fresh flowers and complimentary champaign — unaccustomed as I am to such!)

The city itself is illustrious in its past history. Bristol was founded in the 6th century B.C. by the British King MacImyd and his sons Brennus and Benlinus. Sixteen hundred years later the Domesday Survey ranked it next after London, York and Winchester. Robert, Earl of Gloucester, built the castle at the junction of the Avon and Frome rivers in 1126. William of Malmsbury described the town as full of ships from every port of Europe. It became a centre of African slave-trade, but more nobly it was known for its medieval maritime matters. John Cabot and his son

Sebastian sailed from Bristol in 1497 and discovered the mainland of America, and in the next year explored the American coast from Florida to Newfoundland. It went through stormy times in the Civil Wars and became the Royalist stronghold in the West until Parliamentarians under Cromwell seized the castle.

In 1838 the "Great Western" was launched at Bristol, which was one of the reasons we were here . . . . to celebrate 'bridges and railroads'. I luxuriated at the Grand Hotel while Dick attended meetings, but joined in on the parties. The Church of St. Mary Redcliff was described by Queen Elizabeth I as the "fairest, the goodliest, and most famous parish church in England". There are three good churches and a cathedral. Bristol Cathedral was originally an abbey founded by Augustinian canon in 1142. Where it stands was the traditional site of Augustine's Oak . . . where St. Augustine preached to the British Christians of long ago when England was known as Briton — a tribe, or tribes, inhabiting this area before the Anglo-Saxon invasions — long before it was known as Great Britain. The

13

ancient Britons spoke the Cymric language, similar to Celtic or Welsh.

For a dramatic view of the city approach it from the west. The road suddenly makes a turn and Brunel's great Suspension Bridge is poised 250 feet above the Gorge of the Avon. The verdunt forest on the northern side is like a green ski slope stopping at the river's edge. These are the grounds of Leigh Woods that had originally belonged to Ashton Court. There is much here to explore: Nightingale Valley, Stokeleigh Camp (a triangular Iron Age earthwork) and the site of a disappeared house where Charles II took shelter after the Battle of Worcester. Nature lovers can find many species of mosses and liverwort in Leigh Woods.

Well, every town has its limirick.

> I went to Bristol
> Without my pistol
> Never should a'done such thing,
> For there I saw
> A big jackdaw
> Someone nicked on the wing.
>
> There was he
> In the fork of a tree
> All night a'struggling in pain.
> I went aloft
> So hard I coughed
> It set him free again.
>
> I went to Bristol
> Without my pistol
> And I'll never take it again . . .
> That poor old thing
> With its wounded wing
> I might'a ended his pain.

From *Tot's Verses*, G.R.W.

Now that the convention duties are over we're going to backtrack and visit the beautiful Cotswolds. Although I have given my heart to Cornwall — the spot I hold dearest — I don't feel unfaithful if I admire this fifty miles of lush hills grazed by wooly sheep and criss-crossed by pebbled

14

walls that stretch from Bath in the south to Chipping Campden in the north.

Four miles north of central Bristol on the B4057 you come to Blaise Village. There are about nine lovely gabled cottages scattered around a village green. Though they were built in 1810, they were designed to bring back the rustic quality of a vanishing countryside nostalgia. They had no other for an architect than the great John Nash. Every house varies from its neighbor, as each uses the features of gables, decorated chimneys, crazy hips, and porches in different ways. They create such a picturesque display that the traveller will not want to miss them.

Today there would be a lull in our loose schedule — and like a philosophical fisherman hankering to dangle his line in the old waterhole — we took off just to see what we'd find in the woods. Crossing the Severn River we followed the road to Newent and about four miles farther to the north we came to Dymock, just at the county edge of Herefordshire. Here the manor of Dymock was pointed

The fifty miles of Cotswold hills are populated with many long-haired wooly sheep who thrive on the green lush foliage.

out, and as the story unfolded one of my big questions concerning so many British coronations that I've seen (acted and real) was answered. The name *Dymock* rang bells in my mind and rattled old jousting weapons at the Tower of London, where I had seen the ancient suits of armour hanging with those of Henry VIII's time and earlier. It was this way.

The British Army defeated the Germans at La Falaise, close to Fontenay-le-Marmion in 1944. But this was how it all started. In the mid-eleventh century the Lord of Fontenay was a champion to the Duke of Normandy and followed him to England. For his faithful services William the Conqueror granted him many lands; one in particular was the Manor of Scrivelsby. The family flourished here in the beautiful rolling landsides under the mighty oaks. Their herds were fat and sleek. Sir Philip Marmion, a descendant living on the estate, petitioned for a royal charter to hold a yearly fair and market, and was granted it in 1258. Then, there was no son to carry on his Norman name. But a hundred years later a great grand-daughter married Sir John

16

Dymoke from Gloucestershire and he became the King's champion at the coronation of Richard II (1377). Ever since that event the descendants of the Marmions of Normandy have carried out the duties of 'Champion' at twenty-five coronations — all except those of William IV and his niece Queen Victoria (who excluded that part of the ceremony).

With few variations this procedure has been performed punctiliously. The rituals run thus: when the nobility and sovereign are banqueting in Westminster Hall a fanfare begins; a white horse, clad in all his gorgeous trappings, bears in a Champion in shining armour. Two knights precede him with his shield and spear. The Earl Marshall makes his way for the Champion, while the Lord High Constable rides on his right. The York Herald then comes out to proclaim the challenge to mortal combat to anyone who may deny the Sovereign's right to the throne. The Champion throws down his gauntlet, and the Herald hands it back to him. The challenge is proclaimed thrice, the last time on the steps before the King (or Queen). Next,

Blaise is four miles north of Bristol on the B4057.

the King drinks to his Champion and hands the cup to him
to finish off as he withdraws from the dais.

The present Champion who officiated at Queen
Elizabeth II's Coronation in 1953 was the grandson of the
Champion that served King Edward VII, George V and
George VI. In the novel *Red Gauntlet*, by Sir Walter Scott,
the ceremony of the Champion was distorted, say the
critics.

Dymock has been called a village of the poets, it lies
four miles south of Ledbury, just inside the Gloucestershire
boundary. A Poet Laureate for over thiry years, John
Masefield, a native of Ledbury, describes that area which
each spring turns to a carpet of wild daffodils. He loved
landscapes as well as seascapes. Not only did he have to "go
down to the seas again, to the lonely sea and sky, and all
I ask is a tall ship and a star to steer her by", but when his
heart became tired . . . . it was the "white road westward",
he wrote, "I must tread to the green grass, the cool grass,
and rest for heart and head. To the violets and the brown
brooks and the thrushes; song, in the fine land, and the
land where I belong".

The river Leadon winds its way in and out of the
fields, and their banks become bright gold with the spring
flowers. During the second decade of the twentieth century
Dymock became the haven of poets . . . . one Lascelles
Abercrombie moved into his thatched cottage and wrote:

From Marcle Way
From Dymock, Kemply, Newent,
Bromsbettow, Ridmarley, all the
Meadowland of daffodils seem
Running in golden tides to Ripton Firs.

A partnership consisting of Rupert Brooke, John
Drinkwater, Abercrombie, and W.W. Gibson moved in
together in "The Old Shop", a mile north of Dymock.
They published a quarterly magazine printed in Gloucester
and distributed from the Post Office in Dymock in 1913,
and were going well until the start of the World War in
1914. Then the business folded. A little later they were

Dymock has been called a village of the poets. Here is shown "The Old Shop", the meeting place and publishing house of Rupert Brooke, John Drinkwater, Abercrombie, W.W. Gibson and John Masefield. It is near the county line of Hereford-shire.

joined by Robert Frost where recognition came to him through the writing of *North of Boston*. Soon Edward Thomas found his way to Dymock's pastoral, peaceful beauty.

In the distance was Malvern Hills, bordering the shire of Hereford. There was romance in those slopes. An old dyke can still be seen that Gilbert de Clare, the Red Earl of Gloucester, had marked as a boundary line between his land and the Bishop of Hereford's. I wish we could find the spring somewhere nearby where the poet William Langland wrote his famous long alliterative poem *Piers Plowman*, one of the four greatest writings produced in England . . . . this one coming in the fourteenth century — the other three being *The Pearl Poems* (by the author called the 'Pearl Poet', connected to Edward III's court), *Canterbury Tales* (Chaucer), and the Moral Romances of the Arthurian legends by Thomas Malory. *Piers Plowman* is referred to as a type of 'tract' or pamphlet . . . . the outspoken voice of the commoner and peasant about his plight in the Middle Ages:

In a somer whan soft the sonne,
I shope me in shroudes as I a shape were,
In habite as an hermite unholy of works,
Went wyde in this world wondres to here,
Ac on a May mornynge on Malverne hulles

And as I lay and lened and loked in the water
I slobered in a slepyng —

The vision Langland had was the contents of *Piers Plowman*. No version was printed until 1550, but the fact that about sixty manuscripts still exist testifies to its wide appeal.

In a more recent day Sir Edward Elgar drew his inspiration for the *Oratoria Caractacus* (an ancient chieftain supposed to have lived on Malvern Hills) from this spot.

At this time I think I should say to the uninitiated traveller that nothing I write will cause him to become enthralled with the monuments of any country; I can only steer him toward them and let him develop his own appreciation. I myself got a tremendous thrill upon stepping out for the first time on English soil many years ago. While crossing the Atlantic on the French liner S.S. France I memorized the kings and queens of England since Egbert's time, 827, to Queen Elizabeth II's reign. Then a few basic dates such as: Alfred's translation of *The History of England* by the Venerable Bede (ci. 880); Battle of Hastings in which William of Normandy conquered over Harold (1066); Henry II who caused Thomas Becket's murder (mid 1100s); Henry III, great builder-king (rebuilt Westminster Abbey mid 1200s); Magna Carta signed between the nobles and King John (1215); Chaucer's *Canterbury Tales* (1386); House of York and Lancaster (1461-1485); and most important, Henry VIII (1509-1547); *Translation of the Bible* (1611); and Shakespeare (1611). That will do you for a while. As the cathedrals and castles are visited they will naturally fall in place. It is the best way to study history. Please don't go to England just to stay at the swank Savoy in London, have tea at the Ritz, see the Crown Jewels at the Tower, shop at Harrods, or see Agatha Christy's *Mouse Trap*. And don't think you've seen England if you have taken a guided tour to Windsor Castle or Hampton Court; that's like a foreigner coming to New York City and saying he has seen America —. Oh, that perpendicular metropolis — and you thought only English cathedrals could be perpendicular!

It's not that London is not exciting, on the contrary . . . . it is the most fascinating city in the world. To see a Britisher swaggering along with his jaunty bowler at a precise tilt, staccato cane all trimmed with gold, that pin-striped suit and the proverbial brief case . . . . all sends a thrill up my spine, even though I know that when he gets home he can look forward to few human comforts that we take for granted. His under-sized 'fridge' doesn't make enough ice cubes to cool a glass of tea.* His 'john' responds in a tortured cough when you pull the chain. He will never know what a beefsteak tomato is . . . . nor the coziness of a centrally heated house. But all these luxuries I would forgo for the pleasure of knowing I could go whenever I liked to see the whole panorama of English history and architecture by taking the tube or a taxi to Westminster Abbey, St. James's, the Temple Church of the twelfth century, or just strolling down the street. But here in London too much is missing from the scene: ruins are rebuilt, views of things that existed before the last war blocked out by new edifices, too many foreigners. So to the countryside I'll take myself . . . . into the heart of the Cotswolds.

* That is why all this devotion to 'white' tea . . . . I insulted a publican (bartender) once by asking for lemon and ice!

We leave the Bristol vicinity and are just going to meander along wherever the mood leads. The Cotswolds are situated between the Malvern Hills of Evesham and north of the Kennet River. In the past days this section thrived mostly on stone quarrying and sheep raising . . . you can recognize the area by the repeated use of the greyish-golden stone. We will skirt along northeast of Bristol on the A96 to Dyrham Park near Mangotsfield, which is not much more than a junction for Bath (contains a beautiful church and vicarage garden). A short distance south of Mangotsfield is Dyrham Park, one of the most pleasing stone structures in England. It was designed in 1698 in a combined style of Genoese Palace and English manor house, the facade in warm Bath stone. The interior is not ostentatious; rather there is comfort and a feeling of warmth prevailing—and everywhere blue and white Delftware is plentiful. On the second floor is an unusual collection of Dutch paintings. Since Saxon times there have been fallow deer in the park. The grounds are elaborate with terraces, fountains, parterres, and cascades.

We skipped Westbury Court Gardens close by, as we prefer to go on to Dodington House, toward the north, before it closes for the day. We would find a B.&B. at Chipping Sodbury, a small market place of warm Cotswold stone. Its greatest claim to fame is a 110 ft. column on Nibley Knoll commemorating William Tyndale (1428-1536), translator of the Bible. He was a native of the parish. Two miles south of here is Dodington House. This almost-square Regency-style house was built between 1796-1813, designed by James Wyatt. (In the year of its completion Wyatt was killed when the coach taking the architect and the owner to London turned over near Marlborough.) On the west side is a portico of tremendous Corinthian columns. There are two lakes that flow into a

Northeast of Bristol on the A96 you will find Dyrham Park. It is one of the most pleasing structures in England. The grounds are elaborate with terraces, fountains, parterres and cascades. Shown is the rear of the manor.

22

lower lake, making a lovely cascade. Since 1578 there were Codringtons living on the site (a John Codrington was a standard-bearer to Henry V at Agincourt).

About a mile from Badminton is the splendid Palladian mansion built by the Duke of Beaufort in 1683 . . . Badminton House. The flag was flying from the roof indicating that the family was in residence, so we walked through the grounds to the church containing ducal monuments to the Beauforts (kinsmen of Queen Elizabeth I): Lord Ragland (1855, Field-Marshal of Crimean War fame), and Henry Chardes Fitzroy (eighth Duke of Beaufort). It was here that the game of badminton was begun . . . a sport in which a shuttlecock is batted by a light weight racket back and forth over a net. There were many small ornamental maple trees of many different colours. The annual Horse Trials at Badminton are known internationally; the stables and kennels are open to the public, and also the House at certain times.

One must certainly not miss seeing Berkeley, a sleepy little town of under a thousand persons. It lies about a mile south of the railroad station, and is watched over by a dominating castle. Berkeley Castle is the best preserved specimen of a feudal stronghold (walls fourteen feet thick and heavily buttressed) and with a gruesome history to match its dark gloomy appearance. It was built by the Normans in the twelfth century. Its good condition is due to the fact that only one family has continually lived there since Henry II's reign.

To get into the mood of this house you must know something of its past. Edward II became king at the age of 23. His father Edward I practically died in the saddle trying to best The Bruce and Douglas at Loudoun Hill, only to be defeated by the Scotsmen. Thirty-five years of hard, responsible rule had finished him off. The sad word for England now was that the king's spoilt, handsome son was to occupy the throne. As to Edward II, his first mistake was in recalling his old favourite Piers de Gaveston, against the old king's previous denouncement. The next was not to take his father's heart, as requested, to the Holy Land, but rather to bury him at Westminister Abbey in London. Another strike against him was his lack of military ability to carry on the Scottish and English troubles. But his fatal error was

In 1682 the Duke of Beaufort built the splendid Palladian mansion Badminton House. It was here that the game of Badminton was begun.

Isabella of France. When he went to Boulogne to wed her he left Gaveston as regent . . . one of the highest honours which should have gone to a member of the royal family. Before anyone knew it, a fund of thirty-two thousand pounds had vanished into the regent's embroidered pockets—money that was to have been used for the expense of a new crusade.

England could not long endure this; but in the meantime Isabella had won the English heart by her beauty and also by taking advantage of the baron's, the Parliament's, and the peoples' hatred of Piers de Gaveston. The queen's father Philip IV of France was urged by his daughter to create dissension by forming an opposition party; this was headed up by Edward's cousin Lancaster. The outcome of these arrangements was that Master P.d.G. left England for Ireland—and there was a year's respite from the malefactor.

Later on, in the Civil War that followed, execution after execution took place . . . about thirty in all. Next on the stage of this dramatic period appeared Roger de

Edward I practically died in his saddle trying to best the Bruces and Douglases at Loudon Hill.

Berkeley Castle is the best preserved specimen of a feudal stronghold—and a gruesome history to match its dark gloomy appearance. It was built in the twelfth century by the Normans.

Mortimer, eighth Baron of Wigmore, an ambitious and cruel man idling away his time in the Tower of London. It was about then that Queen Isabella spied this royal prisoner (his uncle, Mortimer of Chirk, sharing his cell, had just died). She had gone there for her accouchement and remained after the birth of her daughter for some time. Her curiosity was aroused by rumours of this attractive resident, and she was as vulnerable as any 'lady-in-waiting'. The opportunity of a meeting finally came; by some hook or crook an escape was planned. Mortimer fled through a hole which had been dug inside his cell into a passage that led to the roof of the Tower's kitchen. From there a rope ladder freed him.

He left for France—so did the Queen of England. Later she arranged to get her son, the Prince of Wales, with her. Her beauty and sorrowful story of neglect by her husband got the sympathy of the French; she easily gathered an army, made of Frenchmen and Low-Country volunteers, and started back to England. To be brief: the result was that Edward II was soon in captivity at Kenilworth Castle — well treated, but completely shut off from his family. He was now just plain Edward of Caernarvon. Meantime, Roger de Mortimer had taken up where Piers de Gaveston left off. Isabella granted him all he previously had lost plus much more. But what to *do* with an ex-king? Could he be a menace? Because of the fear of a *coup* or a conspiracy Edward was sent to Berkeley: there were whisperings about 'the suitable remedy'. Then they discovered two plots for rescuing him, and had foiled both—now it was time for the 'remedy'.

The owner of Berkeley felt sorry for his ex-royal prisoner. Finding it so unpleasant to witness the disgraceful treatment rendered him, Berkeley announced he would be away for awhile. Edward knew the end was near, but he didn't seem to care much any more. No sooner had the owner left than things changed for the worse.

I saw that sinister hole he was shoved into — above the charnelhouse where its vile odors would rise. It was said that even the people in the village below heard shrieks and agonizing screams coming from the castle. They knew what it meant: that King Edward of England was dying a violent death. One account which was widely circulated was that "as soon as the victim was asleep they flung a table over him, which was held down by two attendants to prevent him from moving. The third man then proceeded to burn out his inside organs with a red-hot bar of iron; as it was inserted through a horn, no marks of violence were made on the surface of his body."

Eventually, this poor ex-monarch was laid to rest in a respectable manner at Gloucester Cathedral.

As you walk about this beautiful old castle at Berkeley with pink roses growing on the wall, think about all of this. I wonder if the present occupants ever hear the moans of Edward II's ghost; I surely did that first night when we stayed so close by. (My strong imagination and the wind of course!)

Leaving this sad scene we travel north and turn west at Sharpness on the A4135 for Tetbury. Not much here, just a sleepy little market-town on a hill. Close by is Weston Birt House — a modern mansion containing an important collection of art. The early Gothic Revival church (Mock Gothic) is the best of its kind in England; the box pews smack of an earlier Anglican type.

Now by travelling northeast, the anticipated highlight of our Cotswold tour was to be found near Cirencester. We had, in previous years, followed the flow of the great Thames River from Oxford to Greenwich (east of London), but never knew where it started its humble beginning.

Well, here is the sorrowful and ignoble source of the Thames, that mighty and resplendent avenue of water that gathers power as it moves westward to Reading, Cookham, Windsor, Richmond, London, and finally into the North Sea. But what a mean beginning . . . . and such a contradiction to this lovely section of the Cotswolds. It cannot be reached by boat; it peters out into a tiny trickle as it gets to its head just above Cricklade. So if you want to go there it is best to go by car to Cirencester, then a short distance to the west is the village of Coates. When you reach the church inquire around and be prepared for a landmark shock — even the birds don't peck about looking for moisture — unless there has been a real cloud burst. The old canal there has long been derelict, but by following the towpath about two miles you reach the

Tunnel House, standing forlorn. The only place in all England that you would find a rusty abandoned car would be right here! The tiny issue can be seen oozing by an old fort foundation near Trewsbury House; and down in a meadow in a sunken ground is the starting place of the Thames.

Apart from that disillusion, Cirencester is nice — and really can be called the capital of the Cotswolds. It began about 43 A.D. as one of the chief Roman towns in Southwest England. . . its administrative centre. It was the hub of the network of Roman roads; the Icknield Way, Fosse Way and Ermine Street came together here. Then it faded away until the Anglo-Saxons appeared, who developed it into a sheep raising section. By the 15th century the wool industry was so successful that the wool merchants were able to build a great 'woolchurch'. The parish church of St. John the Baptist is worth a visit. Look for its three-storied fan-vaulted porch, lovely tower and the wine-glass pulpit (a rare Reformation style). Lloyd's of London keep shop in a Palladian building in Castle Street. The Corinium Museum contains fine tessellated ('to lay with checkered work') Roman floors. The only relic left of the mitred abbey founded by Henry I (1117) is the Norman gateway in Grove Lane.

Bibury was on the way to Burford, and I guess that was the only reason for going there. William Morris, well-known English poet and artist, described Bibury as 'the most beautiful village in England'. But then I'd heard that Burford was — and so was Upper Slaughter, as was Ides, and I had a few superlatives of my own — so let's see for ourselves. It's situated on the River Coln and there are some pretty houses of golden Cotswold stone bordering the lovely stream. Near the bridge is Bibury Spring which sends water gushing at the rate of two and a half million gallons a day. Browsing through the churchyard we saw splendid tombs, indicating the town's former wealth in the wool market. On the river to the northwest is the hamlet of Ablington, which distinguishes in my mind the difference between a village and a hamlet — this site was only a cluster of houses and a church. A village is more of an incorporated municipality with certain governing bodies — but smaller than a town.

Continuing eleven miles east on the A433 we find Burford, 'abounding in spandrelled doorways, mullioned windows, pargetted houses'. This will be a good place to stay the night in. Burford lies 20 miles W. of Oxford on the A 40 road. The little River Windrush meanders through, and is crossed by a narrow three-arched bridge. Some of the houses date back to the fifteenth century in their original appearance, others had gone through a face-lifting. I liked the Bear Inn, the Crown Inn, and the Grammar School with its unaltered exterior, built in the fourteen hundreds. The Priory is an Elizabethan structure, but was given a renovation in the early 1800's. Over the doorway is the heraldic arms of the famous William Lenthall, Speaker of the Long Parliament (during Charles I's reign,1640). Near the church is a playing field that used to be Battle Edge where the Anglo-Saxons defeated the Mercians in 752 A.D. The sheep country rises to a plateau that separates Windrush and Evenlode Valleys . . .a place of beauty.

I was looking forward to going to Cheltenham. It was situated on the Chelt river, a tributary of the Severn near the west base of the Cotswold Hills. Visitors are attracted there because of its fashionable health spa. High Street runs a mile and three-quarters east and west. Since 1856 it has been an educating centre. The lovely Promenade leads south to the Montpellier Gardens, and there are also the Winter Gardens and Pittville Park.

In 1716 sulphated and alkaline saline mineral waters were discovered here, and were found to be beneficial for diuretic and liver troubles. It boasts of being a town of 'good taste and elegance imbued with classical culture where people of ample means can come and enjoy themselves therapeutically and luxuriously'.

Students are drawn here by two famous schools: Cheltenham College for Boys and Ladies' College. The Cheltenham Festival of Music is the most important one in the country . . .and it's possible to hear jazz as well as Bach. If this does not appeal then there is racing and cricket.

But we must leave now . . .we'll return when we are "older, with time on our hands?" Winchcombe will be convenient to stay the night — tomorrow Sudeley Park can be visited. Winchcombe is very old and some villagers spoke of the ancient abbey that was started in 797. After a substantial breakfast — even by English standards — we were off to look about the area. This had been the capital of Mercia in Anglo-Saxon times; England then was divided into Essex, Wessex, Northumbria, Mercia and Kent. (So it was rather important.) Henry VIII got the abbey, as he did most of them, but the ruins are turning up some interesting archaeological finds. The Geoge Inn is seven hundred years old and still bears on its door lintels the monogram of the second to last Abbot of Winchcombe, R. Kidderminster.

To the south of the town is Sudeley, the home of Catherine Parr, Henry VIII's last wife. The old ruined medieval castle has been incorporated into the reconstruction of the mid-nineteenth century building. The grounds are marvelous with their formal flower beds, yew trees and pinnacled chapel containing the ornate tomb of Catherine Parr. There are many fine portraits, tapestries, and furniture to be seen inside the manor . . .also all the costumes worn in the movie version of *Anna Karenina*, displayed on wax models. Sudeley was the manor of Lord Thomas Seymour who married the king's widow Catherine. It was this

Thomas Seymour who almost cost Queen Elizabeth her crown because of his *risque* antics when the young princess was living with her step-mother and husband Thomas at Chelsea. When Catherine became pregnant she sent Elizabeth away and the Seymours moved to Sudeley. Here Catherine died in childbirth.

Wonderful memories were to be relived at Tewkesbury. We had been there a dozen years ago. I'd come across the name when I read in Dickens' *Pickwick Papers* that Mr. Pickwick once dined at the Hop Pole with Bob Sawyer and Ben Allen and warmed his coat tail in front of the same present-day fireplace. The literary traveller will want to go to the picturesque mill on the Avon here. Dorlcote Mill has been identified as the one referred to in George Eliot's *The Mill on the Floss* . . . . .and so beautiful it is, with its churning water wheel and high-pitched roof. The rush of the water and the groaning of the mechanics brings upon one a wonderful dreamy oblivion to the world of reality . . . .this day of the nuclear horror possibility. But awake, my love, we must 'make our progress'.

Somehow I liked the sound of 'Tewkesbury' and it stuck with me. On that visit we had stayed at a 'bed and breakfast' with a Colonel and his wife. His hobby was English History. At teatime we were invited to join them before the fire (a weak little flame, but sufficient to cheer the room), and when he learned we were also history buffs, then you know that host and guest were serenely happy. There was to be a *Scn et Lumiere* on the meadow bordering the Abbey and we were given warm army blankets to wrap in, as it was a cold night. The Abbey Church was first founded in 715 as a Benedictine body, then rebuilt in 1102. Although neglect and restoration had taken place since then, it is substantially as it was when reconstructed after the battle at Tewkesbury. It is interesting architecturally, especially the Tower, North Porch and the Choir Stalls. Standing inside one can feel the grandeur of the triforium, pillars, clerestory and vaulting. The great families of Fitz-Hamons, Despensers, De Clares, Beauchamps, and Warwicks are commemorated in the brasses, monuments and stained windows. As is often repeated, most collegiate churches and abbeys which were not ruined by the Dissolu-

Tewkesbury Abbey escaped the dissolution of Henry VIII, as the townspeople turned it into a parish church before he could get his hands on it. It contains the tombs of the great families of Fitz-Hammons, De Spensers, De Clares, Beauchamps and Warwicks.

34

tion became parochial. This one escaped Henry VIII's Cromwell because the townpeople bought the property and turned it into a town parish church before he could lay his hands on it.

The last and bloodiest of the Wars of the Roses took place here, and we would see the enactment of that skirmish on the Bloody Meadow where it happened. During the last stages of the Hundred Years' War that ended in 1453, a marriage was arranged as part of a peace plan.

36

Queen Margaret of Anjou and Henry VI had a son in their
first wedded year. The King seemed dumbfounded at the
great event and only stared stupidly in space. Things
became worse with his mental state. Henry did rally and
return to normal for a short time, but by then there had
developed a political struggle over the Regency . . .then
over the crown itself. The contenders for power were the
House of York (the White Rose) and House of Lancaster
(the Red Rose). As long as the Earl of Warwick supported
the Yorkists they had the upper hand, and Edward IV was
made King, while the demented Henry wandered from
place to place. Finally he was captured and put in the
LondonTower.

But the fickle Warwick decided to change sides —
then the Lancastrians were restored with the weak Henry
back on the throne. Some observers said the King was like
'a sack of wool'. Meanwhile, Margaret and her son Edward
were busy in France while their enemy Edward of York was
in Flanders getting recruits. When the Yorkists returned,
the peace-loving Henry VI greeted them with 'Cousin, you
are welcome.' But Warwick and Edward IV (York), now bit-
ter foes, carried their combat to the Meadow at
Tewkesbury. This was called the Battle of Barnet. Warwick
fell wounded in his heavy armour and died. About the same
time Margaret and son Edward, with troops, landed in the
southwest and started for the midlands — by now all the
Lancastrians were scattered, and young Prince Edward was
dead. The White Rose was victorious and back went the
docile Henry to the Tower. On the same night that the
conquering York (Edward IV) re-entered London, someone
stabbed the meek Lancastrian King. It was never solved —
but many thought Richard III, Edward of York's younger
brother, did the deed. I hope you can understand this most
complicated conflict in English history called War of the
Roses.

It has been a wonderful experience to view this
drama exactly where it occurred. But now it's time to go . . .
and I'm beginning to feel like part of a tour group when I
say that . . . for we generally loiter as long as we like.

In the centre of the Vale of Evesham is the town of
Evesham, a great fruit growing area. Its ancient abbey was
founded in 714, romantically situated with its grounds run-

ning down to the river. Recorded history goes back 1200 years, but here in the Black Wood (legend tells) the Virgin Mary and two angels were seen by a swineherder who was feeding his pigs on the fallen acorns. The local villagers heard of his vision and built a great abbey on the spot in her honour. On the same setting is the beautiful bell-tower standing 110 feet high, built in 1539 by Clement Lichfield. It is considered one of the treasures of England. Also look at All Saint's Church of the 12th century with its gorgeous floral carvings and fan vaulting.

The Battle of Evesham —— there I go again, but I'm tired of apologizing for my love of a locale of immense medieval importance. Medieval Ages began with the fall of classical Rome and lasted until about 1450. The term Medievalism was first used in its modern concept by the Renaissance writer, Flavio Biondo, in the early fourteen hundreds. These medieval times were important to the twentieth century; our government and laws, learning and culture, religion and morals all developed from this wonderful period. The castles, cathedrals, guildhalls testify to the quality of medieval civilization, even though some must do so in their artistic ruins.

So bear with me, it happened this way: Magna Carta was ignored by King John. His son, Henry III, broke nearly all the rules. The barons were determined against this lawlessness and rose in a body with Simon de Montfort leading them. It was not just simply a baron's war this time; all the tradesmen and townfolk sided with Montfort to fight for their rights. They defeated the king in one of the earlier skirmishes, but later Simon was over-come by the Royalists under Prince Edward (later Edward I) in 1265. It was no small affair, four thousand were killed in a fight that lasted only three hours. Where Montfort fell is marked by an obelisk; he is buried in the Abbey.

Three miles N.W. of Evesham is Wood Norton . . . a very impressive English home of the Duc d'Aumale, and much later the Duc d'Orleans. As far back as the mid-eleven hundreds, in Henry II's reign, the d'Aumales had been ruling Northern England with a high hand, but the king put a stop to their pretensions. However a strain of them still hung on at Norton, near Evesham, and Wigmore.

Now we will head for the greatest little 'show case' village in England, Broadway, . . . six miles S.E. of Evesham —— and if you can go in a non-tourist season it will be a delight. It's in all of those 'group packages' that are visited on an abbreviated tour —— along with Hampton Court, Windsor Castle, Oxford University, and Stratford-upon-Avon. For real old seventeen-hundred flavour you will probably stay at Lygon Arms, orginally the White Hart. At an earlier time it was a manor house. Between 1645-51, when England was so troubled with civil wars, the house had given asylum to Charles I. During this period Hunter's Lodge was built and is now a hotel. Projecting wings, dormer windows, gables and chimneys produce a charming picture. To complete the old English atmosphere go for your afternoon tea to the St. Patrick's Tea Room. Almost all of the houses are built in Cotswold stone.

Four miles east of Broadway is one of the most typical towns of the affluent wool merchants, Chipping Campden; it goes back to the thirteen and fourteen hundreds. It was the Roman conquerors that taught the British

39

to spin wool. Later on Edward III furthered the wool industry by bringing over weavers, dyers, and fullers from Flanders (1300's), and three hundred years afterwards Charles II passed a decree that all dead bodies should be buried in garments of wool. The Market Hall in the middle of the main street and the house of Warwick's ancestor, William Grevil, give a good idea of how things looked in the Middle Ages.

To the south of town is a 1487 Grammar School and a stately Perpendicular church. Inside of St. James there are fine brasses of the family of W. Grevil (1400) and others. Permission should be had if rubbings are desired. If you have never done these yourself, take into account the time it requires — a good two or three hours plus the scurrying around for the materials and a donation to the church.Sometimes the verger has done some rubbings in his spare time and will sell them.

Most visitors enter the literary mecca of Stratford-upon-Avon by the fourteen-arched bridge, constructed about 1485. On the High Street Thomas Rogers built a fine house in the mid-fifteen hundreds. Here his daughter, Katherine, married Robert Harvard of Southwark (south side of London), and it was their son John who founded Harvard University at Cambridge, Mass. (1636). Harvard House at Stratford was restored and presented to the University in 1909 as a rendezvous for American visitors.

We tried to find something unrelated to the great Bard — but not much success. Stratford *is* Shakespeare! I guess I am unique in that I like my W. Shakespeare between the covers of a book. And the more I know England, the more I understand his writing. Even in the churches he dominates the place; at Holy Trinity it's the Shakespeare grave with its doggeral inscription that gets all the notice — the visitor generally passing up many monuments deserving of more attention.

There are New Place, Nash's House, and Hall's Croft that are interesting as well as Anne Hathaway's Cottage, the Poet's birthplace, and Mary Arden's House.

Going back in history, there was a Bronze Age civilization here, then an Anglo-Saxon monastery, and later in 1196, the town was granted by Richard I a right to hold a weekly market. The present-day Mop Fair is a carry-

over of those early days and is held every Oct. 12 . . . in the
out-of-tourist season. It celebrates the pre-Tudor period
when farm workers offered themselves for community service. There would be a big Ox Roasting with the mayor and
aldermen presiding over the festivities . . . then country
dancing for all.

I have to be content with a mental picture of the
river at Stratford with the spire of Holy Trinity Church rising above the feathery tree tops, and a three-arched bridge
whose stony body contrasted with the limpid, sparkling
water of the Avon. The sun was wrong for photography.
Surprising that this is the picture I bring home rather than
the image of the greatest poet and playwright the world has
ever known!

About four miles to the east is Charlecote. Sir Sidney
Lee, Shakespeare's most creditable and his last biographer,
writes that the youthful William S. was arrested for killing
deer in Charlecote Park (a great acreage surrounding the
noble mansion of the Lucys of the seveneenth century) and
brought before Sir Thomas Lucy for judgement.

The manor house was built in 1558 and has been
somewhat modernized — incorporating the Lucy Chapel,
inside of which are fine tombs of the Lucy family. There are
footpaths running through the estate.

In the environs of Stratford-upon-Avon are eight little villages connected with incidents in Shakespeare's life;
it used to be possible to take a 'motor car tour' of the
twenty mile area. These are from the Bard's own lines:

"Piping Pebworth, Dancing Marston,
   Haunted Hillborough, Hungry Grafton,
   Dodging Exhall, Papist Wexford,
   Beggarly Broom, and Drunken Bidford."

At *Bidford*, in the Falcon Inn (still there), the Poet
is reported to have caroused to the extent that he had to
'sleep it off' under the crabtree close by; *Temple Grafton*
was the locale of his wedding . . . etc.

It's hard to know when you leave the Cotswolds and
enter the Vales of Evesham or the Shakespeare Country;

oh, what beauty — "Dick, we haven't even seen it for looking so hard. Stop the car!" . . . and we climbed out and walked across the meadow to where an old gate in the heaped-up rock wall swung open. I passed through the gap and saw a deep green valley that seemed to be carved out from a mountain side — with walls sweeping up to the skyline. A bubbling brook oozed out of a crevice and ran on by me growing bigger and bigger as we followed it on its journey. Suddenly it fell over a bluff into a foaming cascade to the bottom. "What an Eden I have found! Let's remain here forever." But the sun wouldn't stay its course, and went plunging on towards its western destiny . . . and we must go, but the lines of Robert Browning came to me:

O, to be in England
Now that April's here, And whoever wakes in England
Sees some morning, unaware
That the lowest boughs and the brush-wood sheaf
Round the elm-bole are in tiny leaf,
While the chaffinch sings on the orchard bough
In England — now!

And I *was* there — and passing it all up by traipsing from one place to another.

But I wouldn't deny the reader the rest of the Cotswolds and their environs. So now to Warwick, Kenilworth, and Royal Leamington Spa. These three are so nearby that we will include them with the Cotswold area.

Lying in the very centre of England on the steep rock cliff above the River Avon is the grandest castle in all Great Britian: Warwick. Because the natural features of its site offered defense advantages it was made a fortified camp. It has an interesting origin compiled by a John Rous, priest (1490). He said that the town of Warwick was destroyed by Picts and Scots and then rebuilt in the year 50 A.D. . . . to be ruined and restored twice more. Arthal, Earl of Warwick, then lived there. Since his name meant 'Bear', and the next owner, Morvidus, had the 'Ragged Staff' as his

Lying in the very center of England on the steep rock cliff above the Avon River is the grandest castle in all Great Britian: Warwick Castle. Some say its origin was in 50 A.D.

device — they combined them to form the heraldic motto of the 'Bear and Staff'. The Saxon came along and made it an important place, but it fell into the hands of the Mercian King. In the eight hundreds, in King Alfred's reign, the invading Danes destroyed the town, but fortunately peace was made with Ethelfleda, Alfred's daughter. She restored what the Danes had destroyed and fortified the defenses with low stone walls and palisades in 916. The castle mound that is now there is of later date, probably Norman, but called by the same name, Ethelfleda's Mound. After 1066 Turchill held the fort, and from him all the present Earls claim descent. In 1068 the Castle of Warwick was handed over to Henry de Newburgh for safe keeping — this family lived there for two centuries. Then it was occupied by Thomas Beauchamp who greatly strengthened the walls and added the Caesar's Tower that so splendidly characterizes the remarkable castle . . .he also built the Gate Tower, portcullis, and barbican.

Richard Beauchamp's daughter, Anne, married Richard Neville (the "Kingmaker"); the title passed on through the Nevilles. The "Kingmaker" was killed in 1471, so the castle was given to the Duke of Clarence (George Plantagenet) who had married his daughter. That accounts for the addition of the Clarence Tower. A few years later Clarence was done to death in London. Some said he was drowned in a butt of Malmsey wine. His son Edward didn't enjoy many days of good living either, as he was highly suspected by the first Tudor King Henry VII and was beheaded in 1499. After him came the Duke of Northumberland, powerful under Edward VI, but attainted by Mary I's Parliament who beheaded him on Tower Hill. The title to Warwick now lapsed until Queen Elizabeth I's reign. She gave it to Ambrose Dudley. About the mid-eighteenth century it came into the hands of the Greville family who still own it. The interior has to be visited . . . a day could be spent here in wandering around the grounds. The most important member of the Grevilles was Fulke (1554), an intimate friend and cousin of Sir Philip Sidney. Dugdale, a Warwickshire historian, writes of the castle,

Charles II on horseback, one of the fine paintings in Warwick Castle.

"not only a place of tremendous strength, but extraordinary delight . . . so that it is the most princely seat within the midland parts of this realm". That is almost two thousand years of the history of that marvelous site standing above the Avon River.

Kenilworth is closely associated with Warwick, not only by its nearness, but its old age, and by the fact that they were both fortifications. One is now a residence and the other the grandest ruin in England. Sir Walter Scott's historical novel of the same title has given Kenilworth much fame. I'm not going into all its origin except to say it was started by Geoffrey de Clinton in Henry I's reign. Years later Henry III gave it to his sister who married Simon de Montfort. After passing through ownership of John of Gaunt it went to Henry IV and remained a royal residence until 1563 when Queen Elizabeth gave the castle to Robert Dudley, her favourite. This period became the castle's most glorious time. Dudley was now Earl of

Leicester and the extravagant entertainment began — such as England had never known.

Scott describes the lavish pageants of its last year very graphically in these lines:

At length the princely castle appeared, upon improving which, and the domains around, the Earl of Leicester had, it is said, expended sixty thousand pounds sterling —

He mentions the pleasure garden with trim arbours and parterres, the complex of magnificent castellated buildings of different ages — the inner court; the armorial bearings of the Clintons, 'time-honoured Lancaster', Montforts, and the Henrys — . Now all crushed under the mammoth ruin.

Everything went beautifully at Kenilworth until Queen Bess discovered her rival, Amy Robsart, in the Swan Tower — then the feathers began to fly! After all, it was she, the queen, who had given it all to Robert Dudley.

There are no two women in English annals who have evoked more fascination than the 'Fair Rosamond' and Amy Robsart. The first was the paramour of Henry II (mid-12th century) and the other the wife of Robert Dudley in Elizabeth I's reign. Rosamond we will take up later when visiting Woodstock.

Edmund Dudley, Robert's grandfather, had been executed in Henry VII's reign (1509) for financial extortions, and Robert's father, John, became Duke of Northumberland . . . rising to power after Somerset's fall during Edward VI's rule (1547-1553). His ambition to put his son Guildford on the throne by marrying him to Lady Jane Grey sent both young people to their execution. (Jane Grey was the 'nine day queen'.) Robert, the fifth son of the Duke had been born one month before Elizabeth I, and had married Amy Robsart at seventeen (1550). Had he not already been wed it might have been he that the ambitious father would have foisted on Jane Grey instead of his younger brother. But Amy was sickly and left alone most of the time at Cumnor House (now gone—but the church close-by has interesting memorabilia) on the Thames near Nuneham Courtenay, not far from Oxford. At court Robert began to monopolize Elizabeth's time more and more—

there was gossip. The Queen ignored such and appointed her favourite to *Master of the Horse*. Warnings came from the Earl of Sussex as he lay dying to 'beware of the gipsy'. True, the friendship between the Queen and Robert was platonic — but not many really believed that. And when it was noised about that she would consider a consort if Robert's wife was not living. . . ironically, Amy Robsart fell down the stairs and died from a broken neck. What people didn't know in those times was that cancer sufferers get very brittle bones and they will sometimes snap for little apparent reason. But the manner in which death had come made a lot of difference with the Queen. Ordinarily — after a period of mourning, the two might have married, but not under the pall of suspicion. She briefly banished him from court.

The destruction of Kenilworth Castle was begun by Hawkesworth and other Cromwellian officers in 1649 — time since has added its aura of romance — and now in its ruinous state has become another monument to the *Commonwealth*.

Leaving Kenilworth on the A452 going southeast we reach Royal Leamington Spa, but one and a half miles from there we would pass Guy's Cliffe, a great curiosity to me. So let's stop for a moment. Romantically situated on rocks rising high above a pool of the Avon River is a house of no particularly interesting architecture. Here, legend says, Earl Guy of Warwick lived like a hermit after "slaying the Dun Cow and the giant Colbrand, and performing heroic deeds in the Holy Land". In the fifteenth century a small chantry was established at Guy's Cliffe and its first priest, John Rous, the antiquary, compiled his famous 'Roll of the Earls of Warwick'. In the courtyard are numerous excavations of relics. Beyond the house are Guy's cave and the chapel of St. Mary Magdalen — the latter containing a disfigured statue of that hero (Guy of Warwick) of the 14th century. The house is mainly 18th century and its walls are hung with Dutch Masters and paintings by Bertie Greatheed, a young artist who died at twenty-two. Mrs. Sarah Siddons (1755-1831), great English actress, lived here as companion to Lady Mary Greatheed.

Not far from the house is the 'Saxon Mill', so often painted by David Cox and others. A little farther to the left rises Blacklow Hill with a monument marking the spot where the 'haughty Piers Gaveston', favourite of Edward II, was beheaded in 1312.

And now on to Royal Leamington Spa, the fashionable inland watering place, situated on the Leam, which is a tributary stream of the Avon. At the end of the 18th century its saline springs began attracting attention. To the N.E. of the town the Royal Pump Room and Baths, with their gardens, may be visited. Many fine Regency houses sprang up on the north side of the River Leam. One can sample the waters free of charge at the Saline Fountain at the bottom of Bath Street under the railway arch. Among distinguished visitors to Leamington were Queen Victoria, Duke of Wellington, Napoleon III, Nathaniel Hawthorne, Longfellow, Sarah Bernhardt and many others.

On the Lillington road, very close to Leamington, is the aged tree called 'Midland Oak'. It has majestic branches spreading far and wide and is claimed to be the *very center* of England. Keats, inspired by it, wrote in "Hyperion":

> These green-robed senators of mighty woods,
> Tall oaks, branch-charmed by the earnest stars.

Going south on the A41 travelling toward Banbury we can expect some nice adventures: Edgehill (about eight miles away), Edgcote House, Compton Wynyates, Upton House, Wroxton Abbey, Chacombe Priory, Sulgrave Manor (so dear to Americans as it was the home of George Washington's ancestors) and several more — all within a nine mile drive.

Edgehill comes into view first. This town was the scene of the first battle of the Civil War, fought in 1642 between Charles I and the Earl of Essex, with indecisive results. A marker indicates the position where Charles's standard was established. About seven miles east is Edgcote House, a Palladian mansion of the mid-eighteenth century. The interior is rococo with good fire-places and plasterwork (can be seen by appointment).

I had missed Compton Wynyates on previous trips, but this time we made special plans to visit. It was no disappointment. The pleasing manor house lies in a hollow of hills that stretch from Tysoe to Edgehill. The structure is a combination of brick, timber and stone built around a courtyard, entered through a door decorated with the arms of Henry VIII. Inside are many rooms, secret passages and hiding-places. In the chapel (part of the manor), divided by a screen, King Henry had a room and a Council Chamber.

Records of 1204 show that Philip de Compton, Marguess of North-Hampton, ancestor of the present owner, pulled down an old house and built this one. The Comptons were loyal to the Crown, and distinguished themselves in battle; one was knighted for heroism in the Battle of Tournai and was presented the grand ruins of Fulbrook Castle. Most of the material used to build Compton Wynyates came from this 'ruin-quarry' — especially the battlemented towers, porch, great hall and spectacular oriel window. There are two fine portraits painted on wood. One is John Talbot, 1st Earl of Shrewsbury who is remembered as the leader of the English against Joan of Arc during the minority of Henry VI. (I consider it a stain on England that when the Burgundians sold the Maid of Orleans to the English that they, in turn, handed her over to the French Inquisition who burned her at the stake in Rouen — 1431). The other portrait is Talbot's wife, daughter of Richard Beauchamp. All through the house are many fine tapestries and paintings.

During the Civil War the house was besieged and captured. The Parliamentary troops had their barracks in the manor. Later the estate was returned to the Compton owners with the stipulation that they fill-in the moat and pay a whopping fine. But the grandeur of the topiary garden with its ornamental shapes alone is worth the visit, without going inside the house.

Sulgrave Manor — how often we forget how deep our American roots grew in British soil! — is nearby. Sulgrave was the home, from 1539 to 1610, of the Washington family before they moved to Brington, a village near Haddon between Northhampton and Rugby. There is a little church there, and on the chancel floor is a stone slab that covers the grave of Laurence Washington, "sonne and heire of Robert Washington of Sulgrave" — who was an ancestor of the famous president. The home, a mile away from the church, still stands.

50

Sulgrave Manor was rebuilt in 1560. In 1914 it was bought by the British Peace Centenary Committee (later known as Sulgrave Institution), restored and equipped to celebrate the 100th anniversary of the Treaty of Ghent in 1814, (merely a victory for arbitration which only swept the problems under the rug). It was not the peace of a victory, no territory had to be won back. United States welcomed it, though, for they had expected to lose some holdings when they sat down to the peace table.

The porch bears the Washington coat-of-arms "a barry of four, gules and argent; on a chief azure three mullets of the second; crest,a demi-eaglet sable rising from an Earl's coronet". It was erroneously accredited as the origin of the "Stars and Stripes" — not so, they say. The museum contains many Washington relics.

George Stubbs, considered the finest painter of horses in England or anywhere, is well represented at Upton House, eight miles northwest of Banbury. There you may see his famous "Haymaker" (dated 1783), and two hundred other canvases by British, Flemish, Dutch, French, German, Italian, and Spanish Artists. This country mansion was built during the reigns of James II and William and Mary. Also look at the tapestries and china collection.

Three miles before reaching Banbury we came to Wroxton Abbey, a 17th century house built on an earlier site of an Augustinian priory of the eleven hundreds — traces can be found of the original structure in the basement. There are many royal treasures to be seen inside including Holbein and Zucchero paintings, embroidered quilts by Mary Queen of Scots, a bed slept in by George IV, and many other objects. The mansion was built by Sir William Pope, who at one time hosted King James I. Later it was owned by the North family, the Prime Minister who was held responsible for losing the North American Colonies. The village is very attractive, with many thatched roofs.

If you have gone to each of these places surrounding Banbury, then you are worn out and ready for a good B&B in this fine old town. There are many medieval streets undulating, twisting, and flourishing in old-world atmosphere. However, it's amazing it is still extant, what with the town's penchant for blowing itself up with gunpowder.

They attacked their own beautiful Norman part-Perpendicular and part-Decorated church in 1792, then rebuilt a new neo-Classical one — which I cared not to visit. There was an old nursery rhyme about the Banbury Cross — well, they got rid of that too; the Puritan thought it Popish and destroyed it in 1600, so as not to 'corrupt' the children. It was replaced with a Gothic Cross in 1859.

Of the two famous inns, only one is left — an American bought one of the 16th century buildings, dismantled it and shipped it home — its mullioned windows, panneled walls, ornate plastered ceiling, and all. The town preserved its three-hundred-year-old recipe for baking flakey cakes and pastries lined with raisins. Isn't that where the "hot cross buns" originated?

Southwest of the town is the lovely Broughton Castle — a moated manor house, dating back to 1300. It had been lived in by William of Wykeham (the bishop who had reconstructed the nave of Winchester Cathedral) between 1324 and 1404. Then it passed on by marriage to the 2nd Lord Saye and Sele, present owners, whose ancestors have lived there since 1454.

Now on to Bloxham on the A361. Long before you arrive, the tall spire of a 14th century church is visible; not only because of its 190-foot-steeple but because of its hilltop elevation. Outstanding features of the church are the circular arched doorway to the west with carvings, and the conopied steps, a 14th century reredos (restored), fine murals, and colourful glass in the east window.

Three miles from Chipping Norton is Rollright Stones, third in importance after Stonehenge and Avebury — almost on the Oxfordshire-Warwickshire bounderies of the Cotswolds. These ancient megalithic monuments of the Cotswolds differ from those in Cornwall in that the former ones are hidden in long, vegetation-covered cairns while in Cornwall they are exposed by 4000 years of wind-swept earth . . . and stand stark on the barren landscape. These are the oldest forms of civilization in England. The Rollright Stones are a group of monolithic circles called King's Stone, King's Men, and Whispering Knights. Authorities say they pre-date the menhirs of the Druids. Nearby are Great Rollright and Little Rollright, two pretty villages; the latter has to be reached by a rough lane through a meadow of unspoiled beauty. These are the places I love to explore.

We were coming to so many towns whose names were prefixed with 'Chipping' — there was Chipping Sodbury, Chipping Ongar, Chipping Campden, and Chipping Norton. I learned it was an old English word for 'market'. Here at Chipping Norton is a Victorian tweed mill that was built in a propitious period to boost the economy of the times. It is adorned with pinnacles and turrets, typical of the 19th century. Where an important castle once stood, now a wool church occupies the mound. The town contains many interesting buildings — the wool market of the 16 and 17th centuries, outstanding Almshouses of 1640, and an abundance of good inns.

On the foundations of an earlier church the Parish Church of St. Mary, of the 14th century, was constructed, incorporating some of the ancient building's features. The porch ceiling is intriguing with all kinds of odd creatures tying up the ribs of the vaulting as though they were ribbons. The interior is flooded with light pouring through the clerestory and the vast area of glass.

From Chipping Norton we go a little NW on the A44 to the village of Chastleton, where there is a lovely Jacobean house of the same name. Robert Catesby, a supporter of Robert Devereaux (Earl of Essex) in a rebellion plot against Queen Elizabeth, was obliged to pay such a heavy fine for the part he played in the evil attempt that he had to sell his house. A rich Cotswold merchant, Walter Jones, bought it. He rebuilt it, adding two towers and five gables and lengthened it into a rectangular manor of beauty and symmetry. There is a secret room where one of King Charles's supporters hid after the Battle of Worcester, while the owner of the mansion got his pursuers drunk so that the fellow could escape.

There are many historical relics and treasures on display; one especially interesting is the Bible that Charles I presented to Bishop Juxon for ministering to him on his execution day. But the nicest feature about the estate is the landscaping with its whimsical topiary yews and old dovecot.

In the vicinity is Oddington, a tiny village with a fine church. (Their pews always provide a time and place to catch up on your notes — surely you don't travel without jotting down.) The Church of St. Nicholas was once a Norman one, but with the palimpsest's skill it is now mainly Gothic. Inside is a shocking 16th century brass representing a former parson in the state of decomposing.

There is a beautiful little city of sharp spires and soft golden stone nestled where the Thames meets the River Cherwell. This ancient spot, Oxford, equally distanced between London, Bristol and Southampton, gradually grew from being a center of political importance to being one of

At Martyr's Corner where Ridley, Cranmer, and Latimer were burned for their Protestant Christian beliefs by Mary I.

55

the greatest Universities in the world. The Anglo-Saxon
Chronicle records that in 912, "King Edward took possession of London and Oxford and all the land which owed
Obedience". Even before the Conquest of 1066 Oxford was
a centre of English Kings and Councils. A hundred years
later saw students and teachers migrating from Paris to
study at the tiny budding clusters of learning groups. A little prior to this, Nicholas Brakespeare — elegant in appearance, discreet in conversation, kindly disposed to all,
rejected by the monastery at St. Albans, left for France and
studied in Paris. He came under the attention of the Pope
and shortly became an English Cardinal. The first one was
Robert Pulleyn — called the father of Oxford University.
Brakespeare went on to be the first Pope elected from
England (Adrian IV) in 1154 — the same year that Henry
II was crowned.

The English 'upper crust' and officiating bodies all
spoke French. The move to have a national language for
common use was hampered because of Stephen Langton,
Thomas à Becket, Brakespeare and others of the ilk. They
tended to run back and forth from Paris and Rome for their
learning and return to England babbling French and Latin.
Nevertheless, a school was growing around the porch and
on the steps of St. Martin's and St. Frideswide's at Oxford
for poor young students desiring to learn. This began to
establish a native tongue of English for England.

Today there are twenty-nine colleges (some list 21,
others 32, but I counted the following:

University 1249,	Balliol 1262,
Merton 1264,	St. Edmund Hall 1269,
Exeter 1314,	Oriel 1326,
The Queen's 1340,	New College 1379,
Lincoln 1427,	All Souls 1437,
Magdalen 1458,	Brasenose 1509,
Corpus Christi 1516,	Christ Church 1525,
Trinity 1554,	St. John's 1555,
Jesus 1571,	Wadham 1612,
Pembroke 1624,	Worcester 1714,
Keble 1870,	Hertford 1874,
St. Peter's Hall 1929,	Nuffield 1937,
St. Anthony's 1950,	St. Hilda's 1893,
Lady Margaret Hall 1878,	St. Hugh's 1886,
Sommerville 1879,	St. Anne's 1952,

It was a harum-scarum sort of curriculum at first, some students living wherever they could and attending classes with any master who would accept them. Then trouble started between the citizens and the scholars — 'town' and 'gown' were forced to part company. This drove the students to seek halls where they could live together with an elected governor — or principal. The Papal Legate began taking notice of the infant University and sent friars to provide good teaching. Colleges were slow developing (they were self-governing bodies of students and teachers), and didn't get organized until the end of the thirteenth century — Merton and Balliol being the first to receive Royal charters. The University was affected by the Renaissance and this somewhat changed the character of the institution. The 'good Duke Humphrey' of Gloucester provided a library which today is the New Bodleian Library, opened by King George VI in 1946 — rather modernistic in comparison with the old Duke's Bibliotheca. When it was completed its cost was a million pounds (before inflation), over half of which was provided by the Rockefeller Foundation. It will hold over five million volumes. To use the books one becomes a 'reader', not a 'borrower', for books may not be removed. Even in early times — though Oxford laid itself at the feet of Charles I and the Royalist cause, the King himself was not permitted to take out even one book from the sanctum of 'Bodley'. Two common little blunders made by visitors are to add the word 'college' to the end of Christ Church (in fact 'college' can be omitted from all but New College), and to pronounce 'Magdalen' as it sounds instead of 'Maudlen'. The omission of the final 'e' distinguishes it from its sister college at Cambridge in printed matters, but they are spoken alike.

At no place was the Reformation found to have stronger influence than at Oxford. Up until the beginning of the fourteenth century the domination of the Dominican and Franciscan friars was paramount. Then came the teachings of the New Learning of the Renaissance through John Wycliffe, Colet, Linacre, More and Erasmus. The shifting of one theology to another finally all but emptied the University for a time. There was the Calvinism of Edward VI's reign (Henry VIII's son), followed by the Marian reaction, then the Elizabethan turn, plus the Civil War

Radcliffe Camera, an Oxford library.

disputes. After the Restoration it settled down to intellectual normality until the Methodist Movement. The years 1919-1920 saw changes: Greek was dethroned, women were admitted for degrees, and government grants were permitted.

The doors of Oxford are always open. Visitors are allowed to walk about at their pleasure. The summer season (mid-June to mid-October) is the best time to come if you are interested in architecture, as the typical University life ebbs then. Sports enthusiasts will find the end of May busy in 'Eights Week' with boat-races and cricket matches; the 'Torpids' are at the end of February, 'Coxswainless Fours' are rowed in November, and the 'Pair Oars' and the 'Sculls' in early June.

Now, an entire book could be written on the University itself, but that's not the purpose of this text, travel is. Oxford should be approached from the east on the London road that leads over Magdalen Bridge, past the school and into the High Street — the most spectacular view in all England. Try to arrive on a Sunday and the town is yours;

58

STEPHEN AND MATILDA WARS

1066 — William I m. Matilda (Flanders)

- Robert (died)
- Richard (killed)
- William II (murdered)
- Henry I m. Matilda (dght. of Malcolm of Scots)
- Adela m. Stephen (Count of Blois) — 1135 Stephen King of England

Matilda m. 1. German Henry V

m. 2. Geoffrey Plantagenet — 1154 Henry II of England

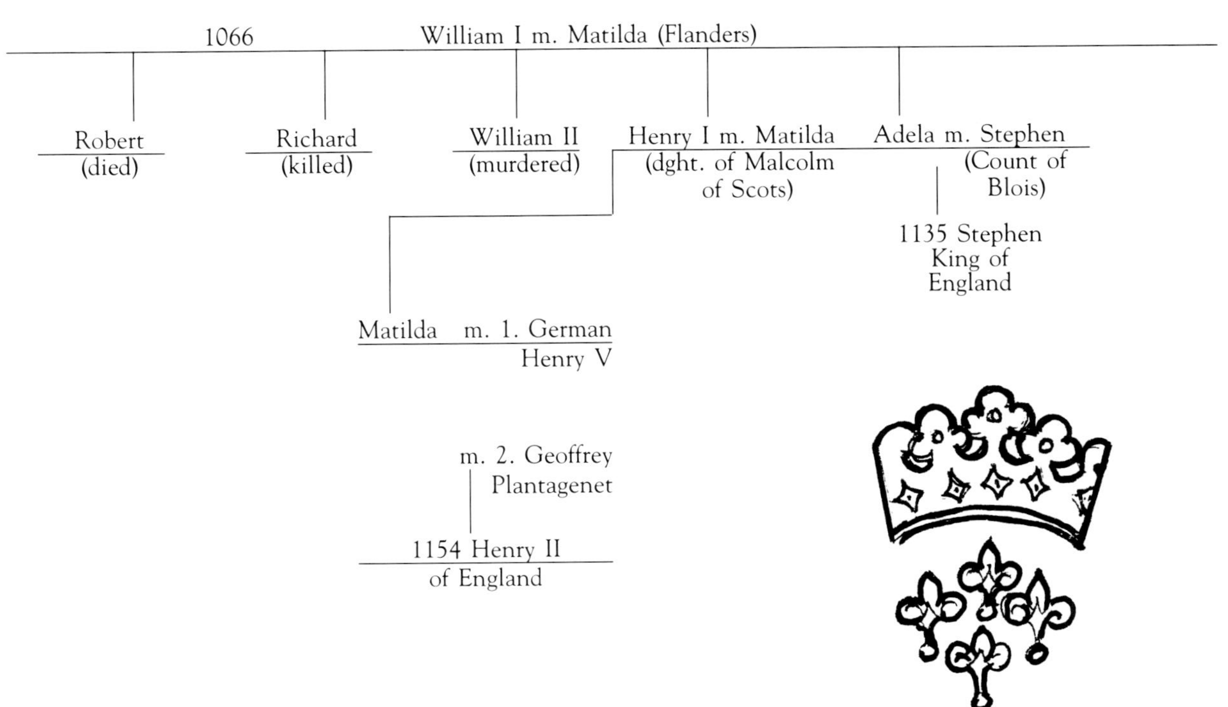

all the industrialists have left for the weekend. The centre of town is Carfax, and it's good to follow High Street to this point and with a city map start exploring from here. The saddest sight in this architectural Eden is Martyr's Corner, reached by the wide street of St. Giles. The monument there commemorates the burning of Ridley, Latimer and Cranmer in 1555 (Mary I's reign). The oldest collection of antiquities in the world is housed in the Ashmolean Museum, built in the middle of the nineteenth century, where there are displays of Egyptian, Greek, Roman, and British treasures. Another site is the castle ruin, of which only the 'motte' and St. George's Tower still remain. The town predates the University of Oxford by five hundred years according to legend, and three hundred by written record. The castle was built in 1071 by the Normans to take care of the developing area, as by then it had become a centre of strategic and commercial importance.

The Isis River runs by the Oxford Castle, and the eleven hundreds witnessed a bit of intense drama. King Henry I's daughter Matilda (grandchild of William I) married the Emperor of Germany, Henry V, and after his death Matilda returned to England. William the Conqueror had a daughter also, who had a son Stephen. He was crowned by the nobles after the English King Henry I died. The Empress (the new King's cousin) didn't like this matter a bit, and wasn't quiet about it . . . so Civil War broke out. It was a time of anarchy and uncertainty, with conflict dragging on for several years. It was while Empress Matilda was staying at Oxford Castle that Stephen besieged it — things were desperate for her. Matilda and a few of her supporters donned white robes and climbed out of a high tower window and descended on a rope into the deep snow. None of the sentries could detect them fleeing through the blinding snow. No woman ever endured such difficulty with the raw elements. The party eventually reached a village where they acquired horses. We found the 'supposed' window and marveled at the lady's gumption.

I doubt that anyone who has been to England has failed to see Oxford, but has he seen the *real* place! I don't know why it is with my husband — maybe the engineer in him — but he always finds his way to the rivers first. There was the Thames; I thought surely it would have made something of itself by now, after its puny start at Cricklade. It seemed as though it was dammed-up at Oxford with junk, clutter of derelict old steamers and rotted wood; it stagnated — while the Cherwell went its merry way,—babbling along under Magdalen Bridge. Folly Bridge, nearby was once named Grand Pont; it had been a Norman one with forty arches. Friar Bacon's study was over one end of it (the Roger Bacon who first put gunpowder to use in England).

Before leaving this jewelled city let's take a little back street to the river banks of Christ Church where the Isis River becomes the Thames. One of the most exiting experiences is to see the ruins of the convent of Godstow where Fair Rosamond was educated, and later buried, 1176. About eight miles southwest on A40 is Cumnor House; here Amy Robsart, wife of Robert Dudley, fell down a flight of stairs to her death.

West of Oxford on highway 40 we reach Minster Lovell, about 12 miles away. But I want to halt a moment before plunging into what I'm afraid has become an

offensive habit of mine: that of telling the reader what he must like or not like — and that he should see this or that. I was reminded of such a practice while listening to Mahler's First Symphony . . . When the first notes poured out it put me in a deep reverie; I saw myself standing on the shores of the English Channel, in Cornwall, looking across the Tamar toward Plymouth. Moving in the reeds I must have disturbed a nesting flock of geese, because there arose in the air a deafening cacaphony of quacking — and a blinding whirlwind of feathers. I was brought to consciousness only by my friend who said, "Listen to the sleigh bells" . . . to which I replied "I thought those were drakes honking". Then I sat back to listen to the Second Movement. And again I drifted far away: the horns and tympanies crescendoed into a forte that seemed to drive the black clouds apart, and a blast of sunlight suddenly lit up the heavens. There, in the harbor I could see the *Mayflower* with all her oars going in precise rhythm and her human cargo swaying at the rails of the ship's sides — some were weeping, some making merry, some feeling foreboding disaster. Then the music became so serene . . . like a calm dawn after a storm at sea. I remarked, "Oh, to be on the Atlantic — with just the balmy air sweeping my face . . ." "No, no, that part is the sleigh flying over the snow in Vienna. I'll give you a book on what to think of while listening to Gustav Mahler's works."

Please don't! You dream your dreams and I dream mine. That is what music is all about — graphic art is a different matter: in it a tree is a tree; a house is . . . etc.

So when you go to these wonderful old places, you think what you want to . . . I'll just tell you what is there. For instance, the family name of Lovell had been haunting me for years. I knew only enough to fascinate me. When we came to Minster Lovell, I couldn't wait to learn more about the ruins. Now, to you it may be just another location — to me, it was part of myself that I was bringing to it and I expected to get something out of it. Lord Lovell, was a sides-switcher like 'Warwick the Kingmaker' who didn't hesitate to shift his loyalty to the area that benefitted his purse . . . as in the War of the Roses. In the 1130's a Lovell defected, along with other barons, when Empress Matilda (granddaughter of William I) returned to England, inciting a civil war. Then the ill-fated Lovell's name crops up again in romantic verse. Later I came across his 'skeleton' somewhere that reminded me of D.du Maurier's story *The King's General* in which Grenville's son starved to death in a concealed tunnel under Menabilly House. It seems that Francis Lovell was implicated in a scheme of Richard III — and after the King's defeat at Bosworth he left the country. A few years later he shows up supporting the pretender Lambert Simnel. When Simnel was exposed at the Battle of Stoke by Henry VII, Lord Lovell vanished into the bowels of his mansion under a heavy iron door that had to be opened from the floor above. He was tended by a faithful servant who brought him food and fresh linen. But the old butler died suddenly — and with nobody knowing of the locked vault — Lord Lovell died very slowly. Two hundred years later workers were making alterations to Minster Lovell and came across the macabre scene: a skeleton sitting at a mouldy table with book, pen and paper whose written contents had long ago deteriorated.

There was another ghastly tale of the house. One of the young aristocrats of the Lovell family brought his bride home on their wedding night. She was playing coy with her bridegroom and hid in an ancient heavy chest which locked accidently on her. Many years later she was found there in the remains of a decayed lace dress.

Today there is less than that left of Minster Lovell — only one wall — on a lovely position above the banks of the River Windrush. You will find it between Witney and Burford.

At Witney, and we're still only ten miles west of Oxford on the A40, we learn that there are connexions here with the Domesday Book. As early as 1085 weaving was a prosperous industry, and here is where the Witney blankets originated. The town is sandwiched between the Windrush river and the wool-bearing sheep hills. Its medieval appearance derives from the Cotswold mellow stone quarried on the site. The Old Blanket Hall, arched Town Hall, and Grammar School are very interesting; the library owns an edition of Homer printed in 1542 with its imprimature, (or license to be printed).

Only a mile's walk NE of Witney is the small village of North Leigh . . . and there on its outskirts we came across a local country man — we visitors are inclined to type them as characters — swinging along, pipe in one hand, walking-cane in the other, and three dogs of in-different breeds following behind. As we approached on foot he turned to see what disturbed his brutes, and seeing us, his face became wreathed in wrinkles and twinkles that made a study in pure contentment. Gone was the need for automobiles, television, the Country Club — everything that mattered was here. I wanted to grab this moment and hold it fast . . . but could not do so. Heaven must wait. I thought of Goldsmith's lines:

> For him light labour spread her wholesome store,
> Just have what life required, but have no more:
> His best companions, innocence and health;
> And his best riches, ignorance of wealth.

North Leigh is a wonderful old Anglo-Saxon place with a part-Saxon and part-Norman church. Inside is en-shrined the lovely Wolcote chantry chapel, and a carved effigy of a knight and his lady beside him. Over the cen-turies these have been kept up by guilds of craftsmen, which gives a sense of continuity to life. Another short walk will take you to a defunct windmill for a romantic picture. In the same direction the remains of a Roman villa with a sophisticated central-heating system can be in-spected. (The roads to it are unsuitable for driving a car.)

From Witney take the A4095 toward Woodstock (8 miles N of Oxford), but first, stop off at Bladon. You will see the Old Malthouse with the lovely faded brick chimneys (just the 'latest thing out' in the fifteenth cen-tury!), and the quaint cottages with mullioned windows. The church here is nothing to brag about — built in 1894 — but the glory of the location is that in the ground lies the body of the greatest hero England ever had: Winston Churchill. His grave is at the headstone of that of Lady Randolph Churchill, his mother, who was Jenny Jerome (an American newspaper publisher's daughter). The simple inscription "Winston Leonard Spencer Churchill 1874 — 1965" is typical of the eloquent statesman who 'thought deeply and spoke slowly'. Standing by his plain slab one can look over the meadow to beautiful Blenheim Palace,

Winston Churchill's grave
bears the inscription
"Winston Leonard Spencer
Churchill 1874 - 1965."

the magnificent edifice of the first Duke of Marlborough, Churchill's famous ancestor. It was written that Marlborough never fought a battle that he did not win or besiege a fortress he did not take. But politics was a different matter, such as Winston Churchill's frustrations in the 1930's with the government affairs. Otherwise, their two careers were very parallel, not only in statesmanship but also in private benevolent living.

Blenheim Palace was built at Woodstock after John Churchill's famous victory at the Battle of Blenheim. In 1704, at a village in Bavaria, Germany, a combat was waged. The gluttonous Louis XIV had wanted to swallow up the Pyrenees — a mountain chain that separated Spain from France. The Grand Alliance made up of England, Holland, and the Empire didn't like the idea — so the bloody matter became the Battle of Blenheim which resulted in the defeat of the French.

Out of gratitude for the victory, Queen Anne granted John Churchill the Royal Manor of Woodstock and a promissory note of 240,000 pounds. As can be expected between two women: Sarah Churchill (John's wife) and Queen Anne had a dispute and 'fell out' with each other

On the A4095 near Wood-stock is Bladon. In the small church cemetery lies the body of England's greatest stateman, Winston Churchill, the simple grave typifying the unpretentious man.

66

— resulting in the Queen's reneging on full payment, which the Churchills were counting on to complete their palatial dream-house. That was a pretty hard financial blow . . . but the Palace survived (a cost of 300,000 pounds).

Woodstock goes way back. It was a royal demesne since Anglo-Saxon times, seeing a succession of monarchs until the end of Tudor days. Henry I (1100) built a manor house and enclosed a vast deer park. It was the birthplace of the Black Prince, son of Edward III; Henry II, his ancestor; and the prison of Queen Elizabeth in Queen Mary's reign. During the Civil War it was practically destroyed. But it is best remembered for its romantic past.

It was not only the setting of Scott's *Woodstock*, but is also referred to in the works of Thomas Delone, a fifteenth century writer, when he penned a captivating description of the *House Beyond the Gate*.

Most curiously the bower was built,
Of stone and timber strong;
One hundred and fifty doors
Did to the tower belong,
And they so cunningly contrived
That none but with clue of thread
Could enter in or out.

This was written about a little liaison in the 1100's involving Henry II and Fair Rosamond Clifford. King Henry was married to Eleanor of Aquitaine, divorced wife of Louis VII of France, but if outside romances between the king and his lady friends ever bothered Eleanor she never protested. This was a relationship that lasted a very long time, as he met Rosamond when he was seventeen, fell in love, and went through the pretense of a marriage service. He then returned to Normandy and was formally married to Eleanor. In his absence a son had been born to Rosamond named William, nicknamed *Long-Espee* or *Longsword*. This son, Henry's favourite, and his mother were housed in the "house beyond the gate in the new wall", called Rosamond's Chamber. Years later, repenting her way of life, she retired to the convent of Godstow. But Henry saw to it that Rosamond was cared for and that

Godstow was liberally endowed. She remained there for twenty years before she died; then Henry had her buried in the finest manner and with candles that would burn constantly.

Let's return to the present. On our first visit we arrived at Blenheim Park too early to go inside, but we were free to roam the grounds. The main entrance to this area is by the triumphal arch a little beyond the church. There are twenty-seven hundred acres in the deer-park, always open to the public. 'Capability' Brown dammed the little Glyme river, erected a column 134 feet high in honour of the great Duke, and elaborated on 'Fair Rosamond's Well'. The trees planted around the column are grouped so as to form the battle plan of Blenheim. It seems that Marlborough's *real* architect was his wife Sarah — of both his fortune and his palace. She was the one who secured a dukedom for him during her early services to Queen Anne, as her companion. When drawing up plans for the building she rejected Sir Christopher Wren and chose Van Brugh's plans instead. The palace is surrounded by long, winding paths and walks covering miles and miles (the number the caretaker quoted I'd be hesitant to repeat — it was so unbelievable). We didn't go inside at this time.

We made a return visit two years later. Take my advice: don't go on Sunday! . . . we stood an hour in line. Notwithstanding, we found it worth the waiting. The sumptuous state apartments contained paintings by Reynolds, Kneller, Van Dyck and others; many *objets d'art;* carvings by Gringling Gibbons; and exotic ceilings by James Thornhill. The ornate marble tomb of the first Duke of Marlborough in the chapel contrasts shockingly with the small poor room where Winston Churchill was born — only a narrow brass bed, rocker, chest of drawers, stingy fireplace and a few framed cartoons on the wall.

Blenheim Palace is considered one of the largest in England, and so ostentatious that it caused Pope to remark:

> "Thanks, sir" cried I, " 'tis very fine,
> But where d'ye sleep or where d'ye dine?
> I find by all you have been telling
> That 'tis a house, not a dwelling."

Blenheim Palace on Sunday afternoon. It is located in twenty-seven hundred acres of deer park that is surrounded by miles and miles of winding paths. Blenheim is considered the largest palace in England. The Duke of Marlborough, John Churchill, was the first occupant.

Despite a close-up look at the stone of Blenheim Palace, tending to make it resemble a bad case of *lichen plantas*, it still is a spectacular sight. The beginning of the eighteenth century coincided with the construction of vast Baroque palaces such as Castle Howard, Chatsworth, and James Wyatt's Dodington House, out-doing their own monarch's in many cases.

We headed our car in the direction of Otmoor, NE of Oxford. This is a rather curious area forming a little ring of villages. Otmoor is spooky — it's supposed to be under the spell of some ancient magic. The first village is Stanton St. John with an old manor house, pretty thatched farms, and a lovely church. The founder of the state of Massachusetts, John White, was born here. The moors can be seen from nearby Beckley — all 4000 acres with hardly an interruption; but somewhere in that vastness was a Roman road that lead to Bicester, which we will explore shortly. In the little church at Beckley the faded wall murals can still be seen. The next small village, Studeley, has thatched roofs and a nice Elizabethan house, Studeley Priory — built over an early Benedictine nunnery. We take the wooded, winding road to a tower called Boarstall which used to be part of a moated castle and continue on to the edge of the moor to Murcott, once the scene of bloody riots that were precipitated by the Enclosure Acts of the 18th century. Enclosures brought about much unhappiness. In ancient Greece and Rome, as well as in Georgian England, the development of the big capitalistic estates ruined the smaller farmer. Fences and tools cost money — they could not exist without their former rights and common lands. So, many had to become hired hands to greedy landlords. Many gave up . . . but the good grazing area is still there. We passed quaint humped-back stone bridges on our way to Charlton-on-Otmoor. The tower of its parish church can be seen from a long distance. An old-world aura hangs over the village, and when May comes there's much to-do with garlands and rural dancing. The place seems to be hiding behind drapings of deep pink wild roses. I had read of Islip, the next town, as being medieval; in fact Edward the Confessor was born here in 1004. During the Civil War three main battles were fought at Islip. Some of the houses are pretty — and make you want to linger. There are three

The rear of Blenheim Palace. Alexander Pope wrote of it:
"Thanks, sir" cried I,
" 'tis very fine, But where d'ye sleep or where d'ye dine? I find by all, you have been telling that 'tis a house, not a dwelling."

71

more villages in the area: Woodeaton, Noke, and Marston — the latter having been the headquarters for Cromwell's troops when they laid siege to Oxford. Hikers will like to stay longer and try the moors.

Bicester (pronounced 'Bister') is about eight miles to the north. It is thought to be a Roman town because of its location on the old Roman road and for its being only one mile from Alchester, where ancient remains have been found. Today it owes its importance only to the Bicester Hunt, which has been popular since the late seven hun-

dreds. The church of St. Edburg's has Anglo-Saxon tracies and is of great interest. Between A41 and A413, tucked away in the Buckinghamshire countryside very close by is Claydon House, a residence since 1463. In 1620 the Verney family took over the lease, it remained unchanged through most of the seventeenth century — as they were keeping a low profile because of their politics during the Civil War. Sir Edmund was an unusual individual; he had been in the royal service when the War broke out, but his religious sympathies were strictly Parliamentarian. Because

The Churchill family at Blenheim: John, Sarah and children.

73

he had 'eaten the King's bread' and served him so long he would not desert him now. "I will choose rather to lose my life (which I probably shall do) — than go against my conscience".

The second Earl of Verney — an imaginative person — left his impression on the manor. He was a devotee of the arts and fond of making a big show. In 1754 the large stable court was added, then the south front extended, followed by the west addition. When the front porch was completed it stretched 250 feet in width, but within a short while after Ralph Verney's death it was diminished leaving the beautiful house only half its size. Its interior is a rigmarole of the most fantastic Chinese decor called chinoiserie. Usually this work is achieved in moulded stucco, but that at Claydon is carved in wood.

There is a suite of rooms where Florence Nightingale stayed on frequent visits to her sister Parthenope, Lady Verney. Cypress trees in the park were supposed to have been planted by Florence from seed she brought home after the Crimean War.

We will drop south on a local road to Waddesdon Manor. In this setting of homeliness one is surprised to come upon this magnificent piece of construction. It is an example of the opulent Edwardian days, built for Baron Ferdinand de Rothschild in the sytle of a French chateau.

The Jew is no newcomer to England. Soon after William the Conqueror, the first immigrants crossed the Channel. They remained until they were expelled by Edward I. Prior to this the Jewish settlers had experienced sometimes favor and other times hostility from the British, but they did thrive as money lenders, as usuary was forbidden as an occupation for Christians. Tolerance, as practiced with the English today, was not followed in those days of the 1100's. For example, recall the cruel treatment of Aaron the Jew of Lincoln, or Issac of York in Sir Walter Scott's novel *Ivanhoe* . . . robbed, beaten, and forced to see his daughter insulted. The day finally arrived when Jewish citizens achieved positions of distinction: Sir David Salomans became Lord Mayor of London, 1856; Sir Moses Montefiore, a leading Philanthropist; and Baron Lionel de Rothschild was a reformer and the first of his race to become a member of Parliament in England. He built his country mansion in Bucks County on 160 acres of splendid parkland in the French style. It includes many treasures from France that were purchased (or stolen) from the Louvre in 1789 while the French Revolution was in full swing, but didn't appear at Waddsdon until a century later. There are Savonnerie carpets, woven near Paris; fine porcelain, paintings by Dutch, Italians, and the English Gainsborough and Reynolds; also statuary by Claude Michel. The Michel (known as 'Clodion') works were collected avidly by Baron de Rothschild.

At Aylesbury, to the west of Waddesdon, we see an old hotel built in the fourteen hundreds. The museum here displays memorabilia of Buckinghamshire history from the 4th and 5th centuries. The Vale of Aylesbury has no distinct boundary . . . but look at the beauty of the area, so rich in pastures and village churches, and you'll know you are in Buckinghamshire. Two miles SW is Hartwell House which was once occupied by Louis XVIII between 1808-14 when he fled France after the first Bonaparte takeover. In 1815 he was recalled to France as King.

Outside of my interest in spiritual growth of man, family responsibility, and national safety — architecture is my great enthusiasm. When you pursue it merely as hobby (as I do) it's a sort of hodge-podge accumulation of knowledge. Isn't it strange that the more refined the state of the art became, the smaller place religion held in the home! In the past — say Pompeii, ancient Japan, China, and Russia — the Altar was the central focus. But as time went on in the western civilization the Great Hall developed and all the family unit shared this for eating, sleeping, and entertainment except the Lord of the Manor — his was a tiny cubicle apart. More time passed; little cells were added for privacy: a solar for the ladies to draw apart, a bower for the other members. When we reach the eighteenth and nineteenth centuries a great house was developing with rooms for cooking, for eating breakfast, formal dining areas, morning rooms, smoking rooms, private boudoirs, billiard parlors (and, my! you should see that one at Halton House close by Hartwell) — but what happened to the Altar? The numerous people occupying the mansion became so private, so withdrawn and selfish, that if they liked, they need rarely ever see the other cousins, aunts, or

hangers-on — so lengthy were the corridors and so widespread the wings of their domiciles.

We are heading due south now on our trek to pick
up the Thames river again. On the way we pass through
Princes Risborough (so-named to distinguish it from Monks
Risborough, a village two miles away belonging to the
Archbishop of Canterbury). There is the Whiteleaf Cross
(80 ft. by 70 ft.) cut into a hill. It was believed that it commemorated a victory over the Danes in 910 — but also
thought to be an intersection marker of the Icknield Way
which joined an Oxford Road in Roman times. A nice
place to stop for tea is in the neighborhood. If it's early in
the day you might rather run over to Amersham because of
its lovely old-fashionedness; in the church there are
monuments of the Drakes whose seat is at the fine Adam
mansion situated in a vast park. Even with all its serenity,
bandits used to lay in ambush for the passerby. The beech
forest was full of marauders. Stewards had to be installed to
protect the people of the Vale.

High Wycombe is Buckinghamshire's second largest
town, dating from Roman days. It has always been a centre
of dissenters — Quakers, Anabaptist and Independents. In
the seventeenth century it was noted for its craftsmanship
in woolmaking, straw-plaiting, and lace-making. It still
maintains its reputation for creating furniture, starting
three hundred years ago with simple chair manufacturing.
The famous 'Windsor' chairs are made there — and the
museum at the Iron Age hill-fort displays almost nothing
but chairs. It's a peaceful place — its air, sky, trees and
brooks proclaim its association with the great poets.
Literary and historical names are numerous: Hampden,
Penn, Burke, Waller, Gray, Shelly and Disraeli all figure in
its annals. And if you stepped aside the way and entered a
cottage you would find the same old lace-making in progress, like a scene in William Cowper's *Contented
Cottager*.

Two miles N.E. is Penn — the birthplace of William
Penn. Benjamin Disraeli lived in Hughenden Manor
another mile away. He was the Earl of Beaconfield from
1830 till his death, 1881. In the churchyard lies his body
. . . and a monument close by erected to him by Queen
Victoria, who considered him her 'dear friend'.

The Georgian home of the great prime minister was built in 1780, but Disraeli was fascinated by the Tudor Age, so had it redesigned in the first distinctive style of English house building. It may be seen on request.

Oh, the Thames is beginning to make a big splash as we move closer to London. We arrive at the little village of Marlow and find a profusion of nice red-brick baroque houses among which is Marlow Place, a sumptuous mansion built for George II in about 1720. These German Georges came over to England after the Stuarts eked out — half-way through the seventeenth century. Elizabeth, daughter of James I — having spent most of her life on the Continent — had a daughter, Sophia, who married into the Hanoverian line; this union later brought forth George I of England. When Queen Anne died, German George's claim became stronger; by now any British connexion was very weak. So here started the 'little Kaisers'. George I married his cousin Princess of Celle, but it didn't last long. Of their two children, one (the boy) became George II — and his father never had learned to speak English. When the younger realized he would inherit England's crown, he began boning-up on the language and visited his future country. He tried being a good Britisher, but he never lost his German accent nor did he give up Sauerkraut and Wurst in favour of Yorkshire pudding and roast beef. He married Caroline of Ansbach, had three girls — all taught to play music by the great G.F. Handel — and two boys, Frederick and William. Frederick died before his father, leaving one son to become George III. But from the history that I've read, there would have been many more wars than there were had it not been for Walpole's restraint over King George II, as he was hot-headed and ill tempered. Well, we all know about George III.

This is Marlow Place of George II's while he was still Prince of Wales, trying to get the 'feel' of the Crown.

Marlow runs down to the river . . . and if I could just think of those lines. Something like this:

> There is a hill beside the silver Thames,
> Shady with birch and beech and odorous pine:
> And brilliant underfoot with thousand gems
> Steeply the thickets to his floods decline.

In this valley there are four natural divisions: the Vale of the White Horse on the north; the Vale of the Kennet on the south; the Berkshire Downs with their attractive villages in between; and the Forest District east of the Loddon River.

The Splendid Astors

If you are going by rail from London to visit Cliveden mansion your train stops at Taplow, then a taxi will take you the two miles there.

No kings or queens were ever served by a more illustrious butler than were the Astors served by Mr. Lee. Royalty called him by name. It is through Mr. Lee we glimpse life at Cliveden of the Astors. The first Astor immigrated from Germany in the last of the eighteenth century. He went to England and then on to America.

Cliveden House is two miles from Taplow on the banks of the River Thames. William Waldorf Astor gave it to his son and daughter-in-law Nancy. In this house the national air Rule Britannia *was first performed.*

78

Whether he himself ever hunted wild animals for their skins is not known, but his fortune was founded on dealing in furs—then in real estate around the New York harbor where the present expensive property developed. His son, William Backhouse Astor, inherited the mushrooming fortune and was called "Landlord of New York", which he passed on to John Jacob II. In 1848 William Waldorf was born—the 'Big Daddy', who became father-in-law of Nancy Longhorne Shaw (Nancy married young Astor, after her disastrous fiasco of a brief wedded life with Robert Shaw, playboy). William Waldorf was known as an eccentric. Americans didn't 'take to' his earning all that money in this country then moving to England to spend it. He purchased Cliveden and also bought the ruined castle of Hever, the 15th century home of Thomas Boleyn's family near Edenbridge in Kent. Astor had been the American Minister to Italy and acquired hundreds of statues with which he adorned the grounds of Hever. This in about 1903. Along with two other town houses in London, he also bought a title from Mr. Lloyd George. His anticipation

Hever Castle, the 15th century home of Thomas Boleyn (Anne Boleyn's father) was purchased by the Astors in 1903.

79

of a son marrying into English peerage didn't come off, for when Waldorf took one look at the American Nancy, peerage held no attraction. When Nancy and the young son of her first marriage arrived in England they were given Cliveden to live in plus two million pounds. Waldorf's new wife was a striking beauty with brains and spunk. She had been the favourite model of her famous brother-in-law Charles Dana Gibson — and was his original Gibson Girl.

Another idiosyncrasy of the older (William) Waldorf was his habit of sleeping with two pistols; he always feared

80

someone wanted to get him. But despite his shortcomings he brought up his son to be the most English of Englishmen. The son showed great love for his wife all through his married life, though it seemed to be displayed more by Waldorf than by Nancy . . . she couldn't reciprocate, rather wasn't able to demonstrate it.

Earlier Mr. Longhorne, back in Virginia, had been hard hit financially, dabbling in many things — night-watchman, piano salesman, railroad worker. They couldn't have been too bad off, though, as Nancy attended a fine finishing school in New York. While visiting her sister, Mrs. Charles Dana Gibson, Nancy met Shaw and married him — and shortly afterwards divorced him. Awaiting legal proceedings she visited Europe and England. She met young Mr. Waldorf Astor who had sailed over on the same ship, and married him soon afterwards in 1906.

By 1928 the Astor household of servants included one hundred and thirty-four employees for their Cliveden, London place, and Plymouth house.

I had not heard much of Cliveden before the Big War, when Lord and Lady Astor did such wonderful work in Plymouth where the Germans blasted that town to pieces. After that, I studied up on them and their estate before visiting it. Possibly it isn't the most famous of the mansions, but its history is fascinating and it's one of the most magnificent country houses in England. Looking down from the terraced porch your eye takes in a full panorama of the lovely expanse of lawn that carries one right to the Thames.

On this site were two earlier manors before 1849, the date of this building. Its architect was Sir Charles Barry who also built the House of Commons. The previous building on the site was the one belonging to the dissolute second Earl of Buckingham, who, after killing the Earl of Shrewsbury in a duel (1668), retired with the Countess of Shrewsbury (the merry widow) to his exotic "bower of wanton love". Also in this house the National Air "Rule Britannia", written by Dr. Arne, was performed for the first time.

After an hour or so of strolling the grounds of Cliveden including the Rose Garden, fascinating Water Garden, the Rustic Theatre and more, we were ravenously hungry and stopped for a delicious home-made lunch served in the Conservatory, Later in the month the open-air theatre would play *All's Well that Ends Well* and in July it would be followed with *Much Ado About Nothing.* There are one and a half miles of stretch, contoured with elms, ash, and beech trees with the underbrush carpeted in wild orchids, devil's paintbrushes and plants I never saw before.

The house consisted of a central block with spreading east and west wings. We entered the Great Hall that was draped in exquisite tapestries. On the south wall hung a life-size portrait of Nancy, Lady Astor, painted by her famous brother-in-law; then to the north we went through the formal Louis XV dining room. I have seen many — but none to equal this. The library was next, with the rare Subicu wood panelling, joining Lord Astor's study. Ascending the carved staircase we were delighted to see that the figure on the first pedestal was an old friend: H. Turberville in full war regalia of William the Conqueror with whom he journeyed from France to England. You will certainly remember *Tess of the D'Urbervilles*—same family—with derelict spelling. Remember the novel. One night, homeward bound from the Dew Drop Inn in a most contented state of euphoria, Tess' father was met by the local historian with a deferential doffing of his hat. He was informed by the genealogist that he had just discovered among some documents that he, D'Urberville, was descended from nobility—that his name was a slight corruption of the famous Turberville. My! what a snob the old sot became after that. Each summer I visit with the very descendants of this Turberville whose name is now Turriville; one cousin got all the treasures—the other got none. Well, here at Cliveden was the Papa of all the D'Urbervilles in a carved wooden statue.

Up-stairs in the gorgeous private quarters of the Astors are the Rose room, the Snowdrop, the Orange Blossom, the Lilac—also the array of nurseries. Over the east wing were rooms for forty guests. To the west were offices and Men's Parlour. Wine cellars, pressing rooms for visitor's clothes, silver safes, polishing sinks, and dozens of other cubicles were in the basement. Little railroads ran through the passageways to rush the food from the kitchen

to the lifts . . . until a more modern system was installed in-cluding hot tables and dumb-waiters. It was quite a distance, alright, for that food to travel in the old days.

As for Lady Astor—the British thought the American bride a bit brash; her maids found her hard to please; the insurance companies that protected her furs, jewels, and motor cars pulled their hair at her peccadillos; but there was no person of importance in Europe who had not feasted at her table. It wasn't until the war with Ger-

84

many came that her heroism rose to the surface. No flightiness in this time of distress; she took off for Plymouth, hardest hit area, rolled up her sleeves and lifted hot soup to the mouths of the wounded men. She and her husband turned over Cliveden to the government as a hospital and Lady Astor became Mayoress of Plymouth as well as first female member of Parliament, which meant commuting by train from London to Devon. By now she was in her sixties.

There was a story told about her that just about sizes her up—personality-wise. During the bombing in London by the Jerries, the Astor's place in St. James's Square received a good share, and much of her ladyship's quarters were ruined. The Astor's turned over their house to head-quarter the Free French Forces, keeping only a small flat at the back for their own use. The rear of their lodging area backed-up to a section frequented by 'ladies' who took their street-corner-Lotharios to cozier accommodations on Jermyn Street. Lady Astor found out about it and turned it into a joke—not that she was given to *ever* telling sexy anecdotes. But it was fun in these strained times to spring it on her closest friends that she was 'the most illustrious lady in Jermyn Street—a real queen of tarts'. One night as she returned home, an American compatriot was stretched out in bliss on the pavement (anything or anywhere was Utopia if it was away from the war horrors for a while); she helped him up and the two struggled along. "Come with me, sonny, I'll fix you up".

"Oh, no you don't; my mother warned me about women like you!"

"Like *me!* . . . I'm old enough to be your granny."

Eventually she got him to bed—the next morning she engaged in what she liked best: to preach on the sins of whiskey and, pressing a five pound note in his hand, sent him flying. She loved drunks, but hated drink.

Well, she was a grand old lady to the end—she and her foolish generosity! She could leave home with a full purse and come back empty-handed to the benefit of scroungers that hung around Eaton Square where she was well-calculated to emerge certain times of the day.

In 1964 Lady Astor was eighty-five years old and very tired, but still with that indomitable will. Following a stroke she went into a coma and slipped away. The Astors sold Clivedon and it was taken over by an American University Extension Center. When the school didn't work out, the National Trust took it under management.

There are so many places to visit in this area—it's hard to pick and choose. This is as near London as we will go for a while . . . and, too, our feet must turn to the west, as in two weeks a visit to Daphne du Maurier is scheduled at Kilmarth in Cornwall. But we are close to Egham, and it has cropped up so frequently in my reading about royalty that we'll just get on the A355, head south and see. Stoke Poges (Thomas Gray's 'Elegy') and Windsor Castle (covered in *Return to Wessex*) lie nearby. The Colne enters the Thames almost at Henley—the right bank belongs to Buckinghamshire and on the left is Egham, above which is the meadow of Runneymede, where the barons met King John, and probably was the actual place where the King signed Magna Carta in 1215—(others say on Magna Carta Island). Royal Holloway College for Women, located at Egham, endowed by Thomas Holloway (a pill-manufacturer in the 1880's), is one of the first female institutes. There is a splendid collection of paintings here and is open to the public. The building is gigantic and fashioned like a French chateau in stone and brilliant red brick.

By dipping straight south and skirting around Guilford, Farnham can be reached in a short time. The Blue Boy Hotel is an adequate place to stop for the night; not only adequate . . . but was necessary in our case. England was having as near a 'cloud burst' as we'd ever experienced abroad—Americans would call it only a light shower. The *cold* was what was killing! It was July. A miniature, shilling-fed heater stood in the fireplace, so we put in a coin or two, crouched close, were able to thaw out our limbs, then sprinted into the blankets. The following day was a heaven-sent one, perfect for exploring.

Castle Street and West Street are the two main thoroughfares of Farnham. Wilmer House and Sandford House are beautiful eighteenth century Georgian homes that can be found on West Street, and the other way takes you up to the Castle. Henry de Blois, grandson of William the Conqueror and brother of King Stephen, built the Norman construction in 1138; it can be seen on top of the artificial mound. Only the *castle keep* remains after Henry II tore almost everything down in 1155 and rebuilt—so what we see now is the second shell. The Bishops of Winchester and Guilford modified it extremely and still use it. The town has a good museum and a lovely park, open to the public. The tomb of William Cobett who was born here in 1762 is in the churchyard. His home is now the 'Jolly Farmer Inn'.

One mile from here is the picturesque ruin of Waverly Abbey. Sir Walter Scott took the name of his first novel from this Abbey, the first Cistercian house in England.

From Farnham an attractive road leads to Hindhead, Haselmere, and Frensham. Now, if you don't care for the Blue Boy-type accommodation you will be happy with the luxurious Frensham Pond Hotel. (Instead of buying that lovely Worcester china tea set you'd spotted to take to Aunt Tillie . . . maybe she'd like the little bag of lavender sachet just as well [maybe!]).

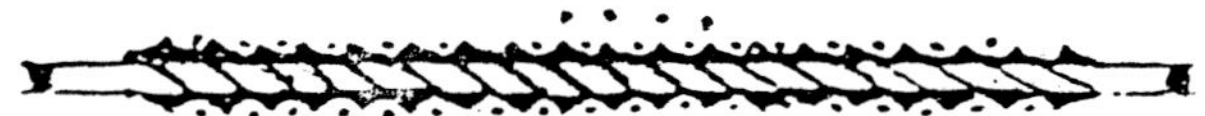

Something's wrong somewhere—I feel no exuberance about this summer's travel. It seems the gusto is gone. I can't relate to my environment. I'm surfeited with overmuchness: too many formal gardens by Capability Brown; too many ceilings of Laguerre; orchestrations in stone by Vanbrugh, scintillating spangles and garlands draping from cherubs by Adams—on and on—. "Dick, please take me back to Devon where the roses aren't scented with some 'numerical Chanel'; waterfalls don't cascade into golden bowls; and tables of malachite aren't presented by Czar Nicholases."

Oh, these are not the real worth
Of this glorious land I've sought,
These are the trappings of the idle rich,
That much unhappiness hath brought.

Man only needs a task to do —
And a neighbor kind o'er the way,
A loving mate by his side,
A God to praise each day.

G.W.

. . . .

Shortly after entering Hampshire we come to Alton. This county is nicknamed Hants—she's famous for the beautiful yew trees. In fact they are so numerous as to be called 'weeds of Hampshire'. Here was once the original Wessex, as it contained Winchester, the ancient capital, the future kingdom of England. We think in more recent times of Izaak Walton *(The Compleat Angler)* and Gilbert White, the artist, in connexion with this area. It was also the birthplace of cricket. I don't know whether Alton is considered a village or a small town . . . its population is about 6000 persons. There is a good restored 15th century church whose south door is riddled with Parliamentarian bullets fired in 1643 during the Civil War. It was located on the Pilgrims' Way. Near the market-place is a house where the poet Edmund Spencer, the 'Poet's Poet', lived in the 1590's.

Jane Austen's home was only a few miles south at Chawton. There is a tablet marking the red brick house where she wrote her most important works between 1809-1817. Her father was a rector of the village. *Pride and Prejudice, Sense and Sensibility, Emma, Northanger Abbey,* and *Persuasion* are well remembered from these years at Chawton.

Fourteen and a half miles from Alton is Basingstoke—a junction between Salisbury and Reading. Near the railroad station is an old 'liten' or graveyard, that came into being after the Interdict of 1207 that closed all the graveyards. Because King John lost Normandy to the

King of France, and all the other Plantagenet possessions, he was called 'Lackland'. He also defied the Pope, who in turn put England under a ban for over six years. No English persons could be buried in holy ground, so this cemetery was set aside for burials. When Archbishop Hubert died (1205), John wanted to fill the vacancy with his own choice, which did not please Pope Innocent III. John refused to accept Stephen Langton, the Pope's man, consequently England was cut off; John was excommunicated. But the King didn't care—he took over the property of the clergy . . . and most all the bishops fled the country. The Pope threatened that if he did not recall the churchmen and restore Godly order that he would get Philip Augustus of France (England's old enemy) to see that John lost his throne. Finally, by 1213 his resistance broke down. He accepted Langton, pledged to repay the clergy, and be a 'good boy'. The Pope lifted the Interdict and the church doors reopened. This before the Magna Carta troubles.

The ruins of the Holy Ghost Chapel (1525) are interesting . . . also see St. Michael, a late Perpendicular example.

Sherborne St. John's is just two miles north from here, where we'd find St. Andrew's Church (1323), much lauded by Horace Walpole.

It was the fourth of July and we approached the lovely old 16th century mansion called 'The Vyne' within walking distance of St. Andrew's Church. The large signboard gave the admission schedule: *Open Wednesdays and holidays.* Never too timid to try a bluff, I rang the door bell. No answer. But I heard voices, so I followed their source. The pleasant proprietor said, "Oh, we're open only on holidays and Wednesdays—this is Tuesday". I replied, "But it *is* a holiday—July 4th; we whipped you in the Revolutionary War in 1783". He gave a chuckle appreciatively, and admitted I had the best of him in 1986 also.

He took us round the back way, introduced his beautiful children, and led us into the main part of the Estate. The Vyne derives its name from a Roman vine-growing villa that was once on the site. The present building was erected in 1500 by Lord Sandys, Henry VIII's Lord Chancellor. Later on, in the 1650's, Chaloner Chute, Speaker of the House of Commons, changed things a bit and added a classical porch. Chute's body lies in the beautiful marble tomb beneath his stone effigy. I cannot

tell you how nice it was to roam about in this fine old place without lots of people around. It was a livable home, remaining in the Chute family until 1956, when it was left to the National Trust by Charles Chute.

To get to Wantage pass on through Newbury in Berkshire. We find that the first factory in England was established here. The prosperity of Newbury goes back to medieval times when a John Winchcombe opened a cloth shop having two hundred looms, employing a thousand women, men and children. Two important battles were fought here during the Civil War in 1643 and 1644. There is a 19th century monument to the 2nd Viscount Falkland. (Lucius Cary), who fell at the first battle of Newbury near Donnington Castle, one mile west. Benjamin Woodridge, the rector of Newbury was the first graduate of Harvard. Then the village of Lambourn, almost joining, leads to East Shefford where John Prince, founder of Princeton University, was rector of the church here in 1619 . . . a very erudite neighborhood, indeed. Close-by is Sandleford Priory, now a school. It once belonged to the Augustinians of the thirteen hundreds. To see it you will have to make an appointment.

On the Berkshire Downs is a remote and peculiar house known as Ashdown, built for the 1st Earl of Craven in the seventeenth century. William Craven was the richest and most valorous man of the age of the Stuarts. Charles I's sister Elizabeth, Queen of Bohemia, returned to England after the restoration, without a husband or a kingdom. William had long been in love with her, with no hope of it ever being a mutual relationship. She had a son, Prince Rupert, to whom Craven presented 31,000 pounds. The silent lover dedicated his efforts to building Ashdown House for Elizabeth, but she didn't live to see it finished; she died at Craven's London residence. He remained a bachelor until his death at ninety-two. A romantic aura hangs over the place, and it's especially felt when viewing all her portraits and memorabilia on display.

Ashdown has a Dutch look about it, and quite out of character stranded on the isolated chalk surroundings. It is four stories high—and taller than it is broad, like an over-size doll house. The outstanding feature is the tremendous staircase reaching from basement to attic and hung with twenty-four portraits.

In 1956 the house was given to the National Trust by Countess Cornelia of Craven. The gardens had become run-down and had lost their original charm, but were restored by the Trust. It is well worth a visit.

Tonight we would stay at Wantage, a thirty minute drive north. Wantage is in the sheltered Vale of the White Horse. This was the birthplace of Alfred the Great in 849. One mile north of here is the parish church of Hanney. The brassies are wonderful; the rubbings make marvelous hangings for the walls of your home. The opening lines of *Tom Brown's School Days* describe the Vale of the White Horse. Several Roman roads come together here . . . the 'Port Way', and 'Icknield Way' are two of them. Three miles away on the chalk hill is the surrealistic figure of a 'home-stretch-bound horse', 374 feet long, cut in the turf. Turned at a different angle it would look like a praying mantis. Since it was created in the Iron Age (though some say at a later date to commemorate King Alfred's victory over the Danes), I can't help thinking that art produced in the modern vernacular has taken a giant step backwards— not only in time but back to the development of a first-grader—as this is how a six-year-old would draw that beast. It may be easily visited from the village of Uffington very close-by. Many think the horse belonged to Britian's Early Iron Age (1st century A.D.) because of the circular eight-acres of surrounding earthworks. But no date is certain on the origin of the Uffington White Horse, something for archaeologists to still work on. Interestingly, a few old hill-horses are being discovered—and though most are white because of the chalky earth—there is a red one near Ban-bury, Warwickshire. It's marvelous the kinds of things dig-gers are coming up with, not just horses but many human figures as well.

We climbed to the top of the hill, but we could never get an entire picture of him . . . in fact the only full view could be seen by helicopter . . . so it must have been for the gods only. Since ancient times there has been devotion shown by the local folk in the festivities held to 'scour' the hill-figure.

At Kingston Lisle, a mile away, in front of the church is a Blowing Stone, a famous perforated sarsen-stone. A

92

clear indentation on the west side of the hill is known as the Manger, and a knoll nearby is Dragon's Hill. A pathway leads to Wayland Smith's Cave. There is a legend about these oddities that Scott used in his *Kenilworth.*

Back to Wantage. There is a beautiful statue of King Alfred in the town center, erected in 1877. The entry passage to the attractive Dutch-style almshouses is paved with knuckle-bones, confirming the plentifulness of sheep in the nineteenth century.

Swindon is a thriving railway town brought to importance by the establishment here of the extensive G.W.R. carriage and engine works. The museum on locomotives is good; one of them on display is *City of Truro* (averaged 70 miles an hour from Exeter to Bristol in 1904); also the *Lode Star* (first passenger train to run from Paddington Station to Maidenhead (1838). One entire room is on Isambard K. Brunel who laid the foundations of the Great Western Railway. At Swindon you can visit the Art Gallery on Modern Art—and the collection on natural history.

Heading West

"Richard, it's time to halt a while before taking in any more ancient monuments". We were just coming to a tiny hamlet—nothing to indicate it on the map—and I spied a little grocer store. I purchased dark bread, tube of mayonnaise (it comes that way abroad), fruit and cheese. The twinkling eyes above the tightly aproned midriff looked up, "Top o'the mornin', Madam". And I laid my selections on the counter. "Two pounds eight pence, Mum . . . and where in America do you come from?" "Alabama", said I, "going picnicing now, but we're staying at the Bear Inn across the road, . . . and, oh yes, cut me off two nice slices of ham—and reach back in your 'fridge' for ones like you've saved for Mrs. 'Plymnickeldalton' ", hoping he'd catch my meaning . . . that I didn't want something he'd pan off on a one-timer customer.

His eyes came near popping out of his head. "Yes, dear lady."

We paid and left. He quickly turned to make an 'urgent' call on the tele. After returning to our room, a message came for Mrs. Woodruff (me) to come to the reception. I faced an over-sized-dove-of-a-little-woman with round black eyes. Her 'pigeon' breast was fluttering so, . . . she could hardly get out the words: "Oh, my gracious, my gracious . . . are you some of Uncle Plym's cousins . . . I heard they were living in Alabama. There was a large clan of Nickeldaltons".

—Gee, I felt like a dunce—and it served me right. But who could possibly have a nomenclature like that! "I'm so sorry", I explained, "it was just a way we have of communicating with our butcher back home . . . 'cept we say 'Mrs. Gotrocks' . . . I thought I was making up such an elegant-sounding name."

Well, after soothing her feathers (oops!. . . .She really was not such a bad old biddy as all that), she wanted us to come to tea at four o'clock! There we met some of her friends, including Mrs. Finch and Miss Lambird. We were still chortling and chirping all the way to Avebury the next day.

Leaving on the A361, passing through Chiseldon, Broad Hinton, and Winterbourne we reach Avebury. "There is no new thing under the sun", says Solomon in the 10th century B.C.—Could these prehistoric stones, set in a geometrical circle, enclosed by a twenty foot bank of chalk, and a great inside ditch cut thirty feet deep, have anything to do with an ancient computer (a forerunner of the Apple C.?) for calculating certain dates—useful to harvest growers! The perimeter of the erect stones—though not as dramatic in their massiveness as Stonehenge—is 1400 ft. The central circle is surrounded by 100 slabs of sarsen rock, native to the area, which is entered by four openings. There is an avenue fifty feet wide bordered with sarsen pairs that leads to the small Sanctuary on Overton Hill, about a mile away.

In the village of Avebury is the Alexander Keiller Museum, opened in 1938 to display the findings of Keiller's excavations. It includes the Sanctuary, West Kennet Avenue, Silbury Hill, and West Kennet Barrow.

The lovely Manor of Avebury is close-by; it's of Elizabethan period.

Well, let' see if Chippenham can better my poor expectations of it, since I knew it to be a manufacturing town situated on the Avon. It also is a cheese and market centre. The seat of the Marquis of Lansdowne is three miles S.E. of Chippenham. The house was designed by the Adams Brothers, which would date it around 1755. There is admittance to the public for the inside where there is an extraordinary collection of paintings by Hogarth, Ruysdael, Reynolds, Murillo, Domenichino, Wouvermans and others. This was Bowood Manor. Three miles south is Sloperton Cottage (near Bromham), the poet Thomas Moore (1779-1852)—not to be confused with Sir Thomas More of two centuries earlier—lived for thirty-five years until his death. His grave is in the churchyard, marked by a Celtic cross. My only acquaintance with the bard at this time was seeing his work *Lalla Rookh* in my father-in-law's library. It was bound in padded wine-coloured leather ornamented in beautiful script and flowers stamped in gold leaf. The charm of its cover attracted me, so it was given to me . . . but I never read the first line of its long volume until I visited the poet's grave. When I did get back to it I found it very lyrical; Thomas Moore, not only possessed the poetic qualities of the bard, but also the truth of the historian. The story, in rhyme, is founded on the fierce struggle between the Ghebers (ancient fire-worshippers of Persia) and their haughty Moslem masters. Moore spent more than four years studying the customs and geography of S.W. Asia, and like Jules Verne, . . . never left his writing desk.

On the Avon, three miles south of Chippenham, is the Augustinian house built for Canonesses in 1232 called Lacock Abbey. It is now a private home and one of the most perfect examples of conventual buildings. It has remained authentic because of the National Trust Act of 1937 (the second one). It enabled the Trust to hold land and provide upkeep of properties that would otherwise haven fallen into ruin. This legislation (the deed held by the Trust) allowed for the restorations and for former owners and their heirs to continue living in the old home. The organization doesn't want these properties to become empty shells of museums, but for the family to make it a viable country home. In 1550 Sir William Sharington brought back from Italy many beautiful Renaissance pieces to adorn Lacock.

William de Longespee's widow had founded the Augustinian convent in memory of him. She became the first Abbess here. It is interesting to know that Longespee witnessed Henry III's *confirmation* of Magna Carta in 1225, it had been signed in 1215 by his uncle, King John, and had been kept at Lacock Abbey until presented to the British Museum by Matilda Talbot in 1944 when the house was given to the National Trust. There has been continuous residence here for seven hundred and fifty years.

In 1540 Sharington added the console window and wonderful Tudor chimneys. William Fox Talbot, the pioneer of photography and a scientist, planted rare trees on the grounds. The first photographic negative ever made had for its subject the small oriel window in the south gallery of Lacock.

If you have poetry interests then you will want to back-track to Calne, four miles east of Chippenham to see where the poet S.T. Coleridge lived . . . also the home of Dr. Joseph Priestly, clergyman and chemist.

Our next town had been on my 'list to visit' for several past summers in England, but it just never quite got done. Sixty-five years ago my uncle, a chemist at T.C.I. in Birmingham, Alabama, had married a clergyman's daughter from Frome, Somerset, England. We found a prosperous looking town with steep narrow streets. In the main one a waterway ran down a shallow trough and disappeared at the end of Cheap Street. This was once a Saxon village in the sixth century. Eleven hundred years later Frome (pronounced Froom) was the scene of brutal executions following the Duke of Monmouth's rebellion in 1634.

We came to the ancient parish church built in the thirteen hundreds. It had been restored and elaborately decorated by W. J. Edmund Bennet. Finding the rector, we inquired about a former churchman, Edmund Bennet, who

96

AFE
The Crusty Loaf
Abbé Hair Stylists
Phone 3604
HAIRDRESSER
FANCY &
A. R. TAYLOR
LEATHER
GOODS
THE
FLORA
RESTAURANT
MODELUXE
DRY CLEANERS

had died about the end of the nineteenth century. He looked up the church records and told us this was the church
and it was he who had erected the 'Calvary Steps' that led
to the north porch. Our mission was accomplished and I
only wish my aunt was still living to see our pictures. Outside the E. end is the tomb of Bishop Ken (1637-1711) who
died at Longleat House, next on our schedule for the day.

Three miles from here was Longleat House.
Longleat!—the 'Treasure house of the West!'—. I couldn't
wait to get there on my first visit in 1970, and was just as
anxious to go there again. We drove through endless roads
of parkland. Wild animals were discreetly and safely placed
for the public to view in a natural environment. Finally arriving at "Heaven's Gate" we could see the cupolas and
chimneys appearing on the horizon, these minaret-like pro-
jections preventing the house from having an absolutely
flat roof. This was the first "country" mansion to be built.
The Marquis of Bath, Sir John Thynne (Thin), set out on
a unique style of country home soon after falling into a
monastic windfall during the Reformation struggles. He
paid a mere fifty-three pounds for the land. It was an age
when church property was tumbling. He began building
this stupendous enterprise—such that Queen Elizabeth
came flying down in her carriage with all her entourage to
see Her Lord High Treasurer's splendid quarters. Hosts
dreaded her summer progresses because of the expense en-
tailed. Some lords estimated that it cost a fourth of their
manor's value to entertain her and her household for five
days. Then a fire destroyed much of the estate in 1567. The
next year the architect Robert Smythson arrived and work
began on the present building. Thynne died before it was
finished. Houses were beginning to use more windows than
ever—'Bess of Hardwick' declared that her house,
Hardwick Hall, would be of more glass than stone. Incidentally, she used the same architect Smythson that Thynne
did almost thirty years earlier.

I always had a soft spot for the east wing of Longleat,
as that was where the outspoken erudite Bishop Ken lived
out his last days. He is not only famous for his courage in
standing up to King Charles II—it seems he disapproved of
His Majesty residing in the same chamber at a local inn
with the infamous Nell Gwynne—and did something about

99

it! He also wrote the Doxology that Protestants sing at every Sunday service. The King held the Bishop in great respect. This brings to mind another good trait of Charles: on the day he died he entreated his brother James to not let "poor Nelly starve". She had been his faithful mistress for many years.

The interior of Longleat contains fine furniture, and paintings by Holbein, Van Dyck, Lily, Kneller, Dobson, Mytens and others.

There will still be time to go to Nunney Castle. The late afternoon sun was on the tall-towered gray stone of the castle built in 1373 by Sir John de la Mare, one of Edward III's greatest warriors in the King's service. It was a gloomy time in England, with the third scourge of plague starting in 1369, along with the Anglo-French wars beginning all over. Many changes in castle building started in the thirteenth century. The perimeter wall was increased because of defense purposes, also the gate towers and corner turrets were enlarged. The old Norman square shape in castle style gave way to the cylindrical form. The builders would have

Sir John de la Mare, one of Edward III's greatest warriors, built Nunney Castle in 1373. By the sixteen hundreds it was reduced to ruins by the Roundheads when Cromwell ordered the building slighted.

to secure a license to castellate. De la Mare had just returned with much booty from France with which he adorned his
castle. It was spared from any attacks until the Civil Wars
of the sixteen hundreds. A story is told that the King's
troops held Nunney when they were besieged by the
Parliamentarians. To show the enemy their great strength
they tortured their only pig every day to make it sound as
if they were butchering fresh meat—and eating 'high on
the hog'. In the end the Roundhead's cannons broke
through the walls, and Cromwell ordered the building
slighted. It's a beauty as a ruin.

A footbridge leads across the village stream to a nearby 13th century noteworthy church. After a quick look inside we will return to Frome for the night, and pick up our
itinerary for Stourhead the next day.

Plan to spend at least a half day at Stourhead to walk
the beautiful gardens and loiter around the ponds and ornamental temples. We had to see it in the rain the last time,
ten years ago. Since then I have learned enough about
gardens to appreciate them and know what to look for. Of
all the gardens in Europe—if I had only *one* to recommend,
it would be the masterpiece at Stourhead. However, we had
chosen the wrong month to see it at its best, as in June the
rhododendrons dominate the scene with their outrageous
scarlet masses (the yellow ones not so obtrusive, though).
The garden here is considered the first natural-landscaped
garden in England, a break away from the geometrical
designs of Le Notre, the French favourite of Versailles'
grounds. There are earlier English gardens of course, but
they are copies of French formal types or sculptured Italian
parks.

The owner of Stourhead, Henry Hoare, planned the
house and garden in the mid-seventeen hundreds. It was
elaborated on and adorned by later family successors. The
main feature of the landscape is the serpentine lake which
lies in a sunken basin surrounded by undulating hills studded with exotic trees and shrubs. There are almost two miles
of footpaths that lead down to the lake, across the bridge,
by the Pantheon, through the grotto and up the hills to the
Temple of the Sun. At the top of Kingskettle Hill (ci 800
ft.), a tall tower was built by the Hoares to commemorate
the Danes' defeat by King Alfred in 879 A.D. The large

cross that you can't miss was made in Bristol in 1300 and brought to its present location in 1733.

There are in England about two thousand gardens open to the public, and the small admission fee either goes to charity or to help with the upkeep of the property. They can be classed in three categories: cottage gardens, landscape gardens, and country gardens. Some belong to the 'keep-off-the-grass' type, some are for day-dreaming in, others are to stroll in. The natural landscape of trees, stones, and water is the most pleasing to me; the botanical kind—with its usual glassed-in-area, fetid aura—the most offensive. I did not mean to write a treatise on horticulture, but there is one garden that I find unforgettable: Sissinghurst, created from an untilled, rough patch of land at the beginning of the twentieth century. It's a show-piece (but excusable in this case); the delight of walking through the 'white garden' of old-fashioned roses with their wonderful fragrance is like magic . . . and the many varieties of topiary yews, tower follies, winding steps, hedged rooms with statues and gazebos are impressive. Oh England, is that why I love you so!

The house at Stourhead is in Palladian style, built in 1722, and has the usual handsome galleries, ornamented staircases, many landscape paintings etc.

I found the 1296 church of St. Peter, built by Henry Stourton, fascinating . The Stourtons owned the land until the seventeen hundreds. The recumbent figure of Sir John Stourton on the tomb inside was carved in 1453. The building had a new facade added when Stourhead was built—the present owner being gracious enough to keep part of the original name.

Edward Gibbons, at fourteen years old, went browsing through the volumes of books in the library at Stourhead and got the idea of writing his *Decline and Fall of the Roman Empire* at that early age. In 1902 the library wing was gutted by fire, and the central part was damaged, but rebuilt shortly, with two wings added to the home.

Rising steeply on one side, on the A303, is a round-table hill and it was believed by many to be King Arthur's Camelot. It was first excavated in 1906, but not too thoroughly. Then in 1913 archaeologists resumed their diggings. They found enough evidence to convince them that

102

there were defenses here during the Neolithic and Iron Ages, the Roman times and even into the Anglo-Saxon period. It was admissible that King Arthur had something to do with it—it was possible for it to have been Camelot, though many scientist say not. The area is vast, and in our walk about it we could have stayed a day longer without covering it all.

Seven miles west of Cadbury we reached Lytes Carey. Nobody seems to write about this place, but to me it was a jewel of a house. A topiary garden interrupted by a gravel walkway catches the eye first. The path leads to a sixteenth century doorway crowned with a lovely oriel window. On the left side is the great hall, built in the fourteen hundreds leading into the chapel that juts out to the front— enhancing the lines of the design. To the right somebody in the eighteenth century had replaced an older gabled gallery with a heavy-looking protrusion that was out of keeping with the rest of the house. For about two hundred years the great parlour was used as a store room for farm equipment, but fortunately in 1907 the original panelling, including Ionic columns, was found in perfect state when all the layers of paint were removed. The 'great chamber', approached by beautiful stone stairs has a marvelous plaster ceiling displaying the arms of Henry VIII—but has none of the spoiling effects of Hampton Court's influence.

I guess what impressed me was the fact that this house was not a 'show-place', but a livable, working domicile where its owners had contributed much to the world around them. In the twelve hundreds and for the next five centuries it was the home of the Lytes. The sixteenth century additions were made by John Lyte, father of the distinguished botanist who published, in 1578, a translation of a Dutch work on "Herbale". This he dedicated to Queen Elizabeth 'from my poore house at Lytescarie'.

None of the labourers paid any attention to us as we walked around the 'white garden', formal pool, farmhouse and stables. Lytes Carey, Clevedon Court and Shute Barton were among the first houses of importance to be built without defenses. (Shute Barton, the home of Lady Jane Grey, nine-day-queen of England, I described in *Return to Wessex*).

104

The day is spent, we're running late to find a nice B&B, but of course the hotels can always put us up. In the area that we are approaching there will be many small manor houses; there is only time for Tintinhull before going to Montacute.

Tintinhull still displays the old stocks that were used to punish village misdemeanors such as a scolding spouse, a wife-beating husband, a false tale bearer—and so forth. It's a pretty old-world village. In 1700 Tintinhull was built in the honey-coloured Ham Hill stone. It was enlarged in 1800, but is still a small elegant manor, surrounded by nice formal gardens. It had its beginning in a modest farmhouse—and was enhanced over the next two hundred years by pilasters of Tuscan columns with a forecourt using piers surmounted by eagles. But it is the garden that most visitors find the chief attraction. Linked steps and sunken gardens give an impression of a greater space than there is. Every species of plants, small trees, grasses and bulbs can be found here, as it was designed by Dr. Price, a distinguished botanist. The best time to visit Tintinhull is in July when more flowers are in bloom and at their overpowering fragrance.

In SE Somerset near the Dorset boundary is the noblest house in England, an amateur brain-child of Edward Phelips, a lawyer and builder. He used the native material, a warm, glowing stone that ages so gracefully. Even though gable matches gable, window duplicates window, and every feature symmetrical—even the smallest clipped yew minutely measured from the mid-front of the porch—it manages to look graceful, and not too formal. This is Montacute House.

There was a conical hill four miles west of Yeovil on the north side of A3088 called *mons acutus*; it gave its name to the village nearby. As time passed it became Montacute. In the fifteen hundreds a Thomas Phelips lived there in a simple house where the present stables are. His son Edward studied law, became successful, was knighted and made Speaker of the House of Commons, later becoming Master of the Rolls. In the year of the Armada (1588) he had begun a magnificent house in Somerset. Houses in those days were a means of expressing one's importance or wealth . . . and this one was all of that! It was fastidiously proportioned, of towering height, and light and airy from the many windows—which were by now very fashionable. The detailed treatment of the obelisks, turrets, and pavilions made it a poetic composition in stone. In the seventeenth century the Phelips lost out financially, and the house retired into a quiet country home—giving up its ambitions of being an imposing monument to wealth.

The only change in Montacute House was in the switching of the entrance to the west side, constructing a two-

story wing to accommodate passage-ways, and adding more convenient features for comfort. The porch is a most attractive mixture of Renaissance and Gothic architecture resulting in a lovely eclectic structure.

The interior is surprising. The long gallery (the main feature of the Elizabethan and Jacobean mansion) is the longest one of that period to survive; it now displays the marvelous collection of early sixteenth and seventeenth century portraits from the National Portrait Gallery. There are some splendid five-hundred-year-old Tournai tapestries and

In S. E. Somerset near the Dorset boundary is the noblest house in England, Montacute House. It was begun in the late fourteen hundreds by Thomas Phelips whose son studied law, was knighted and became Speaker of the House of Commons and Master of the Rolls. It was he that brought the house to its present magnificent appearance.

107

fine Gobelins on exhibit. The grounds are magnificent! (I believe I said I was tiring of all this falderol—but it seems I'm not—think it was only because of impatience to get to my old haunts in Dorset, Devon, and Cornwall—and we're practically there!)

With an early start in the morning, we can make it easily to Sticklepath by late afternoon. There are many accommodations in Ilminster on the A303, about six miles west of Montacute.

Ilminster, an industrial expanding town, has some nice places to visit. The best would be the fifteenth century church with a wonderful tower, patterned after Well's Cathedral, beneath which you will find most of the Wadham family reposing 'neath splendid brasses. It was Dorothy and Nicholas (died 1609 and 1618) who founded Wadham College, Oxford. The George Hotel has a plaque that boasts: First hotel that Queen Victoria ever stayed in—(at age seven months).

It's a beautiful day and my heart is beating wildly, for in a few hours we'll be at the Farm in Devon and we will sleep in the same place every night for two weeks. Honiton

My heart beat wildly for the simple beauty of our favorite dwelling . . . Forde Farm, dating from the Domesday Book.

is the next town on the A303, which we usually bypass, but will visit later from the Farm. When you approach Exeter look carefully for road signs to find the A30. I have covered the city of Exeter in the first two books of the 'Trilogy', so will not comment here. However there's one place closeby that we've ignored over the years . . . a little village just on the outskirts of Exeter. There is a sign pointing to Ide. For an old world atmosphere stop for a cup of tea and a scone; I'll return next week and loiter all I like, but now on to Cheriton Bishop ten miles away. Another six miles to Whiddon Down, and three to South Zeal, then Sticklepath!

It was a real 'going-home' feeling when we drove down the lane to Forde Farm. The Youngs, the dogs, and the cats all having been greeted, we went to our room to hang up our clothes that had been suit-cased for three weeks—then out for a walk. The sky was a soft violet blue seen nowhere but in southwest England; the ford, that had been the ancient boundary line since the Doomsday survey, was populated with a new flock of ducks. Roses over the gate made a solid mass of yellow and their perfume permeated the area. This would be our fourth summer here.

Supper was at the Seven Star Inn; we would order soup with bread and butter, then a shrimp cocktail. Mr. Maynard, a goldsmith, had recently bought the inn as his home, and it would continue to accommodate the public. A crowd was gathering outside the windows, we paid our bill and joined the group of spectators to watch the Morris Men. In talking with the entertainers we learned that their fathers and their fathers' fathers since the middle ages had belonged to this Wessex Company.

That night we sank into a deep, buoyant mattress

under four blankets, while the air blowing in from the moors
billowed the curtains into a horizontal stance.

The next day was to be taken leisurely. We would drive
to Lewtrenchard for lunch, though where I'd put it, what
with that breakfast I'd consumed—well, the food was worth
toying-over just to see the inside of the loveliest, most livable
home in Devon. Sabine Baring-Gould spent most of his life
in the beautiful manor house, between Lydford Castle and
the village of Lewdown. To get there we'd take the A30 from
Sticklepath on through Okehampton and another six miles
to Bridestowe; keep west for six more miles and Lewdown
is reached. From here turn left on a local road, almost dou-
bling back (inquire if you like—we did at a grocer store). . .
one mile down the road you can't miss it. I am telling you
all this because it hasn't made the tour books yet—it is still
unspoiled.

Driving up to the entrance of Lewtrenchard, you first
notice the fine wrought iron gates that are always open to
greet guests. In Henry II's reign the Trenchard family were
living in the manor. (Think of it: 1180's!. . . and they later
acquired Wolveton, near Dorchester). The Monks of
Potheridge received it through marriage, but Thomas Monk
ran into debt in the early sixteen hundreds and a Henry
Gould purchased the estate, the family of Gould still holds
the deed. Many generations of Goulds lived here, but the
most famous was Sabine Baring-Gould, author of countless
numbers of books, sermons, and articles. He was also a hymn
writer; best known are "Onward Christian Soldiers" and "On
Resurrection Day".

The most beautiful room in the manor is the Banquet
Room in Wedgewood blue embellished with stunning white
sculptured plaster work. Wander over the Minstrel Gallery,
Long Hall, and the Conference Room. It is an inn now, and
most reasonably priced.

Be sure to visit the little Lewtrenchard church almost
joining the manor. Leaving there we decided to explore—
so we kept going south on this country road and arrived at
Marystow where we examined the lovely old church. From
there to Chillaton and, turning eastward to North Brentor,
we headed for Lydford for tea. We knew from previous stops
here that we would run into some pleasant country talk and
gossip. (These are not parts that tourists go to—so you will

*The manor of Lewtrench-
ard started in the reign of
Henry II . . . 1180's. It ran
into debt and in the early
sixteen hundreds it was
purchased by Henry
Gould. The family of
Gould still holds the deed.
The most famous of the
clan was Sabine Baring-
Gould, author and hymn
writer — Onward Chris-
tian Soldiers, for example.
Observe the plaster work
in the dining room.*

get good service and will experience real rural life *au naturel*. For our earlier experiences in Lydford see *Return to Wessex*.) By now the day was coming to a close and we headed for the Farm.

Tomorrow we would go east beyond Exeter to Beer, near Seaton Bay. It would be a long day—an eighty mile drive. Now I know that's nothing in the States; many people commute that distance to their jobs every day—but here, it is something else: you want to mosey along looking for little oddities.

From Exeter to Clyst St. Mary is five miles to the east. It was here that the Prayer Book Rebels were shattered with clubbings and hangings. Edward VI had introduced (1549) the Prayer Book in English, which action had riled the Cornish Catholics. They marched to Exeter, which they besieged for five weeks . . . until they were worn out and bested by the local townsmen. Passing through Woodbury we reached A la Rondo—a peculiar octangular building of Victorian days, containing many collections of mundane items. Then on to Exmouth (ten miles east of Exeter), a town with plenty of accommodations, a resort at the mouth of the

Exe River. Steamers can be taken to Bournemouth, Dartmouth, and Salcombe. I can't get away from these tourist havens fast enough—so on to Budleigh. Here you may visit the beautiful Bicton Gardens one mile north. They were designed by the French Andre Le Notre, the master of Versailles' landscaping. The hilly village of Budleigh has thatched cottages running up and down-hill with brooks spanned by foot bridges. Sir Walter Raleigh (1552-1615) was born at Hayes Barton, a mile north. There is an interesting group of various bench-ends in the little church and a memorial to the Raleigh family. Next is Sidmouth, a beautiful seaside resort. The Royal Glen Hotel was once Woolbrook Cottage where the Duke and Duchess of Kent brought their young daughter (later to become Queen Victoria). There are walking paths that lead up to some fine views atop Salcome Hill Cliff.

The next village is my type of place. Branscombe has houses of cob and thatch that climb up the woodsy slopes. From here, there is a three mile walk to Beer with splendid scenery. And now we reach Beer, a small fishing village in

At Exeter we attended the Sadler's Wells Royal Ballet. Exeter citizens like to boast that they are the last outpost of civilized living in the West Country. We saw <u>Swan Lake</u> with Galina Samsova and David Ashmole dancing the leading roles.

a tiny bay. Once it lamented a dark and sinister past of evil smugglers. Beer Head is the westernmost chalk cliff along the entire Channel coast (423 ft. high). The Old Quarry was used until the late eighteen hundreds; it went back to Roman times.

We will turn westward here after getting a bowl of soup and sandwich at Colyton. Colyton is in a rich farming vale; as early as the seventh century the Saxons tilled this land. You can decide between two castles if your time is limited; the castle of Shute Barton is two miles north. . . or to the south is Blackbury Castle. Shute Barton was the home of Lady Jane Grey, the sad little victim of a proud father-in-law's royal ambitions. I couldn't find out anything about the other one, so passed it up. Now a hasty retreat to our 'dear haven on the moor'.

What a wonderful day we awakened to. We greeted our host at the breakfast table; she had a harrowing incident to relate. The evening before, on returning home they encountered a very cluttered scene. After ascertaining they had not been burgled—no signs of forced entry—they discovered that jackdaws had found their way down the chimney and had themselves a real wrangle. They ran wildly back and forth among her antique vases and plates—even knocking over sugar bowls and tea pots. There were feathers everywhere . . . on the cupboards, the window panes and stuck to the old hand-hewn beams supporting the ceiling. All was quiet now and back to normal.

We asked to make a long distance call to Cornwall, as we were to tell Dame Daphne du Maurier's secretary that we were free any day that suited her schedule. Our date was set for cocktails on the following day. After hanging up the phone I, woman-like, went into a dither — what to wear! I was so excited I couldn't think of planning on going anywhere today. So we just went up on the moors above Okehampton with a picnic lunch and to do nothing. It wasn't hard to find the right spot — squatty cypress trees shaded the area, aromatic with the fragrance of wild flowers and cedar. There are always polyester laundry bags in the car that we use to spread on the ground. As this was army base property, open to the public, we dared not make a fire to heat tea, but found that orange juice is not bad at natural temperature. Some baby sheep timidly crept up to us followed

114

by their mamas who soon became nuisances.

It was a day never to be forgotten. I brought a copy of Richard Ford's *Gatherings from Spain* to browse through. Next to my over-powering love of England, I rate Spain as second best. The name of Richard Ford comes up sooner or later in travel books on Spain. Ford was a well-to-do Englishman, fortunate enough to be able to take his ailing wife to a warmer climate when the doctor prescribed it. He was a close friend of Washington Irving, whose *Conquest of Granada* was published in 1830. He was also on friendly terms with Henry Unwin Addington, then the British Minister at Madrid. Ford remained in Spain in the pleasant surroundings of his wife, three children, three maidservants and prominent companions. In three years he learned to speak Spanish perfectly, dressed Spanish and adopted their customs. He knew Spain better than any Spaniard knew his own country. A few years after returning to England, to Exeter, he died at age sixty-two. I laid the book aside, closed my eyes and was 'out of it' for a dream or two. Waking up, I found Dick had the same idea — and the left-overs of our noon repast had been consumed by the wooly young

Dick sleeping on Dartmoor —his idea of the perfect vacation.

*See page 118 for
Spanish—English lineage.*

scavengers who took off on their four little legs with a
bah-bah-bah.

It was time we took off too. Driving back to our
quarters I began musing over Ford's writings about the
Spanish people and realized what it was that Spain and
England had in common; it's their natural courtesy and
politeness to visitors. And if you trace the history of each
country you will find many other features in which they
relate. Spain's greatest ruler was Isabel the Catholic; it's
sobering to think that Isabel's grandmother on the mother's
side was Philippa, the daughter of John of Gaunt; her paternal grandmother was the other daughter of Gaunt, Catherine
of Lancaster. So the blood of Spain flowed down to the
English Henry VIII and his daughter, Queen Mary, stopping
there.

Kilmarth, Cornwall

Long before meeting Daphne du Maurier I had become
acquainted with her through her books. I had pored over
the settings of each novel with maps—had visited the greatest
number of them. I even knew of her ancestor's beginnings
before the turn of the eighteenth century.

. . .   .

January 5th, 1827

"At ten minutes past nine
o'clock last night in Rutland
House, Arlington Street, died
His Royal Highness Frederick,
Duke of York and Albany, in
the 64th year of his age."

116

Mary Anne Clark, fifty-two, picked up her London Times and read the simple announcement of her old lover's death. She had been banished from England and was now living in France after nine months of confinement in King's Bench prison (in conditions that would make a London slum seem like paradise). Because of scandals implicating a member of the Royal family, namely the Duke of York—and many other notables, and the long litigations pertaining to her involvement in forgery, she was in disgrace.

Mary Anne had two daughers—Mary and Ellen. Their mother's hope was that they would marry 'belted earls'—or men with money—or just *men!* They came along, alright—but not just what she anticipated: Mary's fellow, Bowles, loved awhile and left her; and Ellen . . .well, she got her Frenchman with his phony title, who called himself Busson du Maurier.

We are concerned with Ellen, Mary Anne's daughter.

Ellen Clark married Louis-Mathurin Busson du Maurier. Earlier, the father of Louis (Robert Mathurin Busson) had suffixed his name with du Maurier, designating his descent to be from a well-to-do French family that lived in the ruined *Chateau Maurier* near the western coast of France. This he did when he became an emigré to England during the Napoleonic Revolution (as he was a supporter of the King) with the idea of impressing the English foreigners. Actually, at this time *Maurier* was only a simple farmhouse belonging to a glass-blowing family near Vibraye.

Ellen and Louis Busson were living in Paris (1844) where he was a 'budding' inventor of a portable lamp. The young couple knew nothing of their respective French and English backgrounds until his new-found aunt (through a fortuitous meeting) writes the entire history of his ancestry and sends it to him. This letter constitutes the book, *The Glass-Blowers*, by Daphne du Maurier. I recommend it for its historical references and geographical interest, centered around Bellème, la Ferté, Ferté Bernard, Le Mans, Mondoubleau, Vibraye, Montmirail and Vendome. My husband and I had travelled through all these places and felt affection for that part of Brittany, France.

Of course the nephew, newly discovered, was crestfallen to find himself *'crestless'*—no motto "Abret ag Aroag"—no descent from old knights of Brittany. "Then

SPANISH AND ENGLISH MARRIAGES

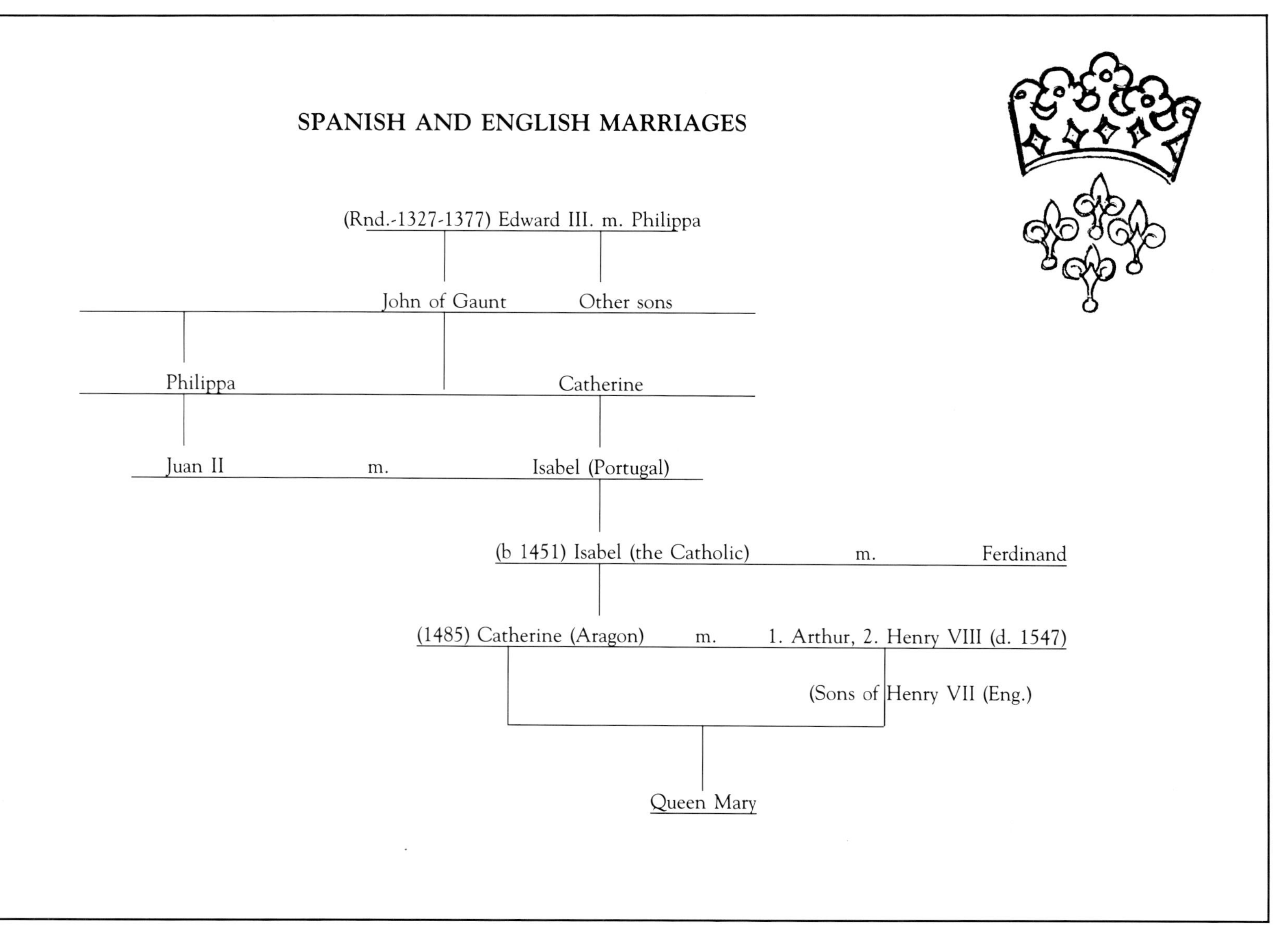

PATERNAL   MATERNAL

Pierre Labbe   Thompson

Marthurin Busson   m.   Magdaleine b. 1725   (Psuedo
                                             du Maurier)   Mary Anne Clark 1796

b. 1764 Sophie (Duval)   b. 1749 Robert-Mathurin Busson m. Maria F.

b. 1793 Zoe M. Rosiau   Louis-Mathurin Busson m.   Ellen Clark

b. 1834 George (Kicky) du Maurier d. 1896   m.   Emma Wightwick

(1873-1934 Gerald du Maurier   m.   Mauriel Beaumont

Daphne b. 1906   m.   Frederick Browning (Lord)

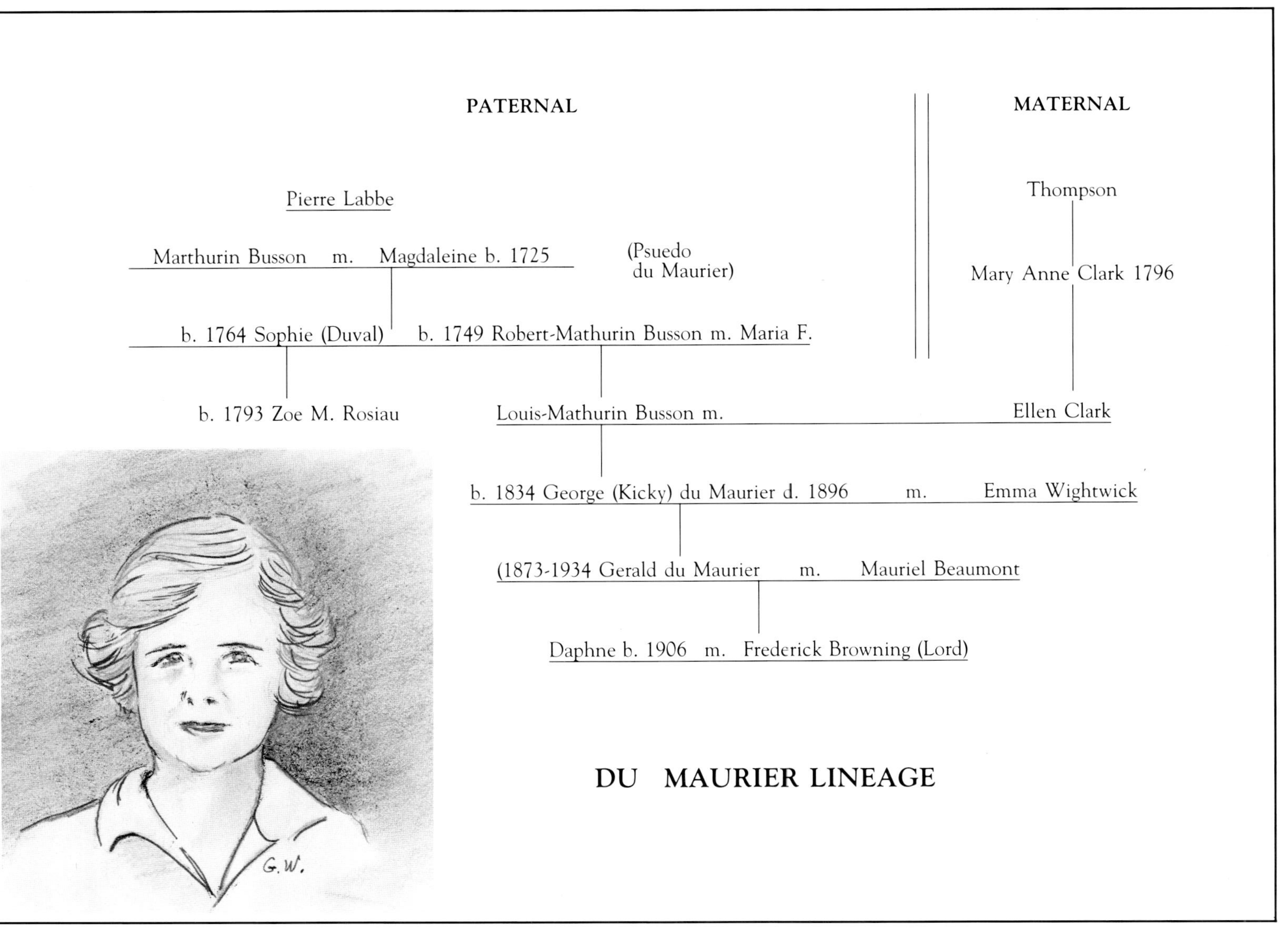

DU   MAURIER LINEAGE

none of this is true", says he to his Aunt Sophie Duval.

"Your father Robert was first and foremost the most incorrigible *farceur* I have ever known," said she bluntly— "but I loved him."

To Louis-Mathurin Busson du Maurier and Ellen Clark a son was born; they named him George (1834)—nicknamed Kicky. He was a lad of ten when his Great Aunt Sophie met him in Paris. When she looked in his eyes he looked back at her with the very eyes of her own brother. There was no doubt now; this was her brother Robert's family. Sophie presented the long-cherished goblet that had been preserved in a leather case these many years to young George and told him, "This glass was made by my father, Mathurin Busson, on the occasion of the visit of King Louis XV. My father used to say that as long as it remained unbroken the creative talent of the Bussons would continue. There," she said to the boy, "stay true to your talent—but if you abuse it, as my brother did, the luck will run out of the glass."

The talent of this young George was drawing and writing. He married Emma Wightwick around 1860—who wielded a mellow influence over him. Later (1865) he became the illustrator of the respected and beloved *Punch*, weekly paper published in London. He was only thirty-one, but in mid-middle age he wrote three novels, *Trilby, The Martians,* and *Peter Ibbetson,* based on real life experiences embroidered in plots that were absurd and melodramatic. But how the reading world loved them! George du Maurier's fame became widespread—but he was contented to be a man of simple pleasures, with just a bit of nostalgia for the beloved Paris of his childhood. His personality radiated warmth and trust, attracting people with this sincerity. And if any man never had an enemy it was he. Hampstead Heath, in the northern part of London, became his home, where his son Gerald was born. Those who knew George claimed that he was nothing short of a genius—and on top of that to be graced with a beautiful voice!

Daphne and Gerald du Maurier

Gerald du Maurier, the magnificent actor, was born in 1873. When he was thirty-three, in 1906, Daphne was born. There were three girls: Angela, Daphne, and Jeanne (the youngest). Daphne became her father's favourite . . . perhaps her rich imagination that manifested itself at an early age caused a bond between father and daughter, also because she was so much like her grandfather, George, Gerald's father. The actor made his first big success as 'Raffles' in 1905—a play filled with action from beginning to end. The Edwardian audience was delighted with the fast moving pace of the piece. The women went wild over the hero who played a subtle burglar—a regular gentleman, not a villainous fellow easily detected. He handled his gun with all the grace of one lighting his cigarette in fashionable society. The critics were impressed—this was a new style on the stage. Then there was the role in *The Ware Case*, which continued to fill the Wyndham Theatre. Now came an opportunity to combine theatre management with acting.

His three daughters were fascinated with grease paint and watched him apply his faces. Gerald had met their mother, Muriel Beaumont, during their acting together in Barrie's *The Admirable Crichton* in 1902. There was mutual adoration from the first and continued on through life. And when his eyes occasionally roved to a new young acting partner, Muriel had the grace and good sense to close her eyes. There was one incident later that opened them wide, though. The children never heard any of the reverberation, but Daphne's father came to his favourite daughter and whispered, "Mummy is very angry with me—I don't know what to do." The Father-child relationship was very close throughout his life.

In 1917 Gerald du Maurier's finest acting came to the fore in Barrie's best play *Dear Brutus*. By now du Maurier had founded a school of natural acting—but it didn't mean that there were easy steps or short cuts to becoming a great star. Of course it never hurt the young 'idol of the matinee' that his father, George, had just been published and become an immediate success in England and America with his *Trilby*.

Gerald received a Knighting for his theatrical contribution in 1922. His name was synonymous with 'Bulldog Drummond'. At fifty he was still youthful enough to co-star with Gladys Cooper in *The Last of Mrs. Cheyne* by Freddy

Lonsdale. There are many more plays I could mention, but that is not my purpose at this writing. I have given the barest possible background to introduce you to my beloved novelist, *Daphne du Maurier.*

After crossing the Tamar River at Plymouth you are in Cornwall—land of mystery. Cornwall is, correctly speaking, a 'duchy' and not a county (or shire). The eldest son of the sovereign is always the Duke of Cornwall—and for that reason you will most likely come across the Prince of Wales there than any other part of the country. We did on two occasions: but only once were we close enough to shake hands with . . . when he was visiting the prison on Dartmoor at Princetown, only six miles from the Devon-Cornwall boundary.

More than four centuries ago Cornwall was visited by the Greeks. "The Cassiterides," mentioned by Herodotus as yielding tin," undoubtedly included the peninsula as well as the Scilly Isles." Long after England became Saxon Cornwall remained Celtic, and the Cornish language did not become extinct until the 1750's. It still survives in personal names and places in the frequently recurring prefixes of Poe, Ros, Tre, Caer, Lan, and Pen—all meaning pool, heath, dwelling, town, church, etc, respectively.

An hour later we turned off the main highway 390 just before reaching Lostwithiel to look at Restormel Castle, of the thirteenth century, one mile away. Lostwithiel had been the capital of the Duchy seven hundred years ago. Restormel was the best fortified castle in its era than any in those parts—some of it dating from eleven hundred. It was abandoned for many centuries until the Parliamentarian forces occupied it in the Civil War, 1644, when Richard Grenville's men drove them out. Read *The King's General* by du Maurier for more information on this area.

After crossing the Tamar River at Plymouth you are in Cornwall (a 'duchy', not a shire or county).

122

I.K.BRUNEL
ENGINEER
1859

*Prince Charles and Lady
Di.*

Daphne du Maurier

A few miles from here was Tywardreath (another frequently mentioned locale of du M.'s *The House On the
Strand*). This town was so familiar to us that we didn't stop,
but hastened on to St. Blazey, then off the 390 to Par, the
shopping area for the neighboring villages. Just a breath away
we drove through the open gates to the grounds of Kilmarth.

124

This was the second home of Daphne du Maurier *Browning*. The first one was Menabilly, about a mile down the road . . . a house she had 'found' as a child while exploring in the woods above the Gribben headland. She fell in love with the place at a very early age and couldn't shake the infatuation. Later on she got permission from the absentee owner, Dr. Rashleigh, to wander about the grounds. Gradually she pieced together its history. There was the ghostly lady in blue who peered from the window—and the young cavalier that was found under a buttress when the house was remodeled in 1824. Menabilly played a big role in the Civil War—in fact the King's gold was brought from a boat in the harbour, then through a tunnel into a storeroom beneath the manor, where nearly two hundred years later, the skeleton of the young man was found. He was supposed to be the son of Richard Grenville.

Years went by—the young writer spent some time in France, and in England at Cannon Hall, Slyfield Manor near Esher, Cumberland Terrace in London, and Soulsbridge Cottage near the border of Buckinghamshire; but finally she came to terms with her inner self and satisfied her love for the sea when she found solitude at Fowey Harbour in Cornwall. She was being published by this time. It was 1929 and the novel was *The Loving Spirit*, followed by *I'll Never Be Young Again*. Living at a remodeled boat house called Swiss Cottage at Bodinnick, near Fowey Harbour, she undertook to do some garden clearing and while pruning trees she was struck down with appendicitis. It was now 1931. A major in the Grenadier Guards, Boy Browning—second in command to the battalion of his regiment—, had just read a book by a girl down in Fowey, not far away. It was *The Loving Spirit*, and his pleasure from its reading made him want to meet the author.

Her sister Angela first spotted the attractive man in the white motorboat through her field glass. Daphne took a look. "H'm," she said, "he *is* rather good." A year later found her married to this Boy Browning. It was the simplest ceremony possible—they went by boat to the little Lanteglos church where the heroine, Jane Slade, of her first book was buried in the churchyard.

Boy Browning became General Sir Frederick Browning and she Lady Browning. Also she was awarded the title of Dame Daphne du Maurier for her literary

The village of Tywardreath is frequently mentioned in du Maurier's The House on the Strand *and* The King's General. *It is located near Par and Kilmarth. Daphne du Maurier lives at Kilmarth.*

TYWARDREATH PARISH CHURCH
DEDICATED TO
ST. ANDREW
SUNDAY SERVICES
7.15 a.m.   MATTINS and LITANY
8.00 a.m.   HOLY COMMUNION
11.00 a.m.   HOLY COMMUNION
11.00 a.m.   SUNDAY SCHOOL (IN THE HALL)
6.00 p.m.   EVENSONG (1st, 2nd, 4th and 5th)

THERE IS A CELEBRATION OF HOLY COMMUNION
ON WEDNESDAYS AND GREATER HOLY DAYS AT 9.30 a.m.

accomplishments.

After rearing her family at Menabilly, which she revitalized after securing a lease for 26 years, the Rashleigh owners decided to reoccupy their old manor again. The Brownings moved to Kilmarth, about a mile away.

I remembered in her collection of short stories and memoirs (published in 1980, called *The Daphne du Maurier Notebook*, which she had given me the summer before) she had penned one essay "A Winter's Afternoon, Kilmarth" in which she wrote of the half hour succeeding lunch—after a full morning of unnecessary letter-writing—she could sit back and enjoy a cup of black coffee and smoke her first cigarette of the day. The papers were still unread, but she donned her 'Tolstoy' outfit (as she called the over-large coat, fur cap with ear flaps, rubber boots, padded jerkin etc.) and set out for a walk to the coast below her house. The weather was raw—even her West Highland terrier Moray, after taking one sniff of what he'd be feeling beyond the porch, darted back inside. She urged him on and they trudged along through the sloping field that was under plough, with dung globs left by careless South Devon cattle. But this had to be traversed to reach her destination . . . to walk along the sea. She told of her tortuous moments when the weather became more than mortal man relished—but calmed herself by thinking of all the places she'd rather *not* be: . . . such as ringing doorbells of people she scarcely knew but whose invitation to cocktails she had begrudgingly accepted . . . the door opening to a blast of cacophony from the already arrived guests; the hated standing in fitting rooms of smart London shops squeezing herself into some outfit that would be 'just smashing' for a shindig she'd rather avoid accepting . . . or how about circling an airport waiting for the fog to lift! But nightmares aside now. The little haven of security provided by the overhanging stone was now in the path of a Niagara that was forming higher up from the downpour. And now the same mud field had to be recrossed to reach Kilmarth again.

O, reader, I wish I could convey the nostalgia I feel for this place. Here is Dame Daphne standing in the Victorian porch of her slate-shingled house that stood above the foundations of the home of Roger Kylmerth who lived here in 1327 . . . and I'd like to make Time stand still so I could

Tea time at Kilmarth with Lady Daphne du Maurier Browning. Mementos of her famous actor-father, Sir Gerald; her grandfather George, novelist; and close friend The Queen Mother may be seen on the mantle and window ledge.

wander around the place, and touch the walls of the base-ment which used to be the main structure, with an overhead loft for sleeping accommodations—this now being the eleva-tion of the main floor to the present building.

My previous contact with her was during her con-valescence after a bout with pneumonia—and then only from her window, where she had risen from bed to speak with me. I thought I'd never get over *that* . . . But now this: cheek to cheek in embrace. And you thought the English were stiff and undemonstrative!

We entered the long room—or drawing room — on the right of the hallway, opposite the dining room and library. The French windows gave way to the garden that was enclos-ed by a wall topped with iron railings. Before arriving, I wondered what on earth I would talk about when I was in her company—but now words came spontaneously. The two West Highland terriers tried to absorb her attention, but their jealousy was rewarded with a confinement elsewhere. The house breathed with comfort and cheer. On the mantle was a jar that contained paintbrushes . . . I supposed them to

130

have belonged to her grandfather George du Maurier, artist
and writer of renown.

My hostess was offering me my choice of drinks. (What
did I care . . . swamp water would have been acceptable). We
sat side by side on the sofa, and the conversation turned to
family. I 'just happened' to have some snapshots along—.
Meantime Dick was given permission to roam about with
the camera.

Daphne du Maurier is a beautiful woman. The bright
blue eyes were emphasized by the azure coloured turtle-necked
sweater she wore. But if you passed her on a crowded street
you'd never remember her apparel . . . whether sable or
hopsack—. But those eyes! Even more than her writing, they
spoke of worlds of seas, castles, sadness, joy . . . life itself.

I took in all the memorabilia round me: the statue of
her actor-father, photo of the Queen Mother (her personal
friend), the *Sunday Telegraph*, bits of this and that, old
portraits on the wall . . .

It was a polite time to rise and go. An embrace, French
style, and off we went . . . with singing heart! And yet I've
told you nothing of her—this du Maurier . . . the embodi-
ment of a hundred persons: a woman with prowess at the
helm of a boat, a poet, a mother, a writer, a dreamer, a lover
of one man, and an humble soul who knelt each night to
her Creator, "Give peace in our time, O Lord. And may
those who by Thy counsel lead the peoples of this earth give
a right judgement."

At age twenty she wrote these lines:
> Mine is the silence
> And the quiet gloom
> Of a clock ticking
> In an empty room,
> The scratch of a pen,
> Ink-pot and paper,
> And the patter of the rain,
> Nothing but this as long as I am able,
> Firelight—and a chair, and a table.

From "The Writer" (1926)

Esther Rowe, her companion, walked with us to our car—and for you to visualize her loveliness you must know her. She has three grandchildren and manages to look like a college girl. She must know more about her companion than anyone will ever know about Daphne du Maurier. We left through the iron gate and turned into the Tyrwardreth-Par road that would take us to an intersection known as Four Turnings. I immediately recalled the last lines of du M.'s *My Cousin Rachel.*

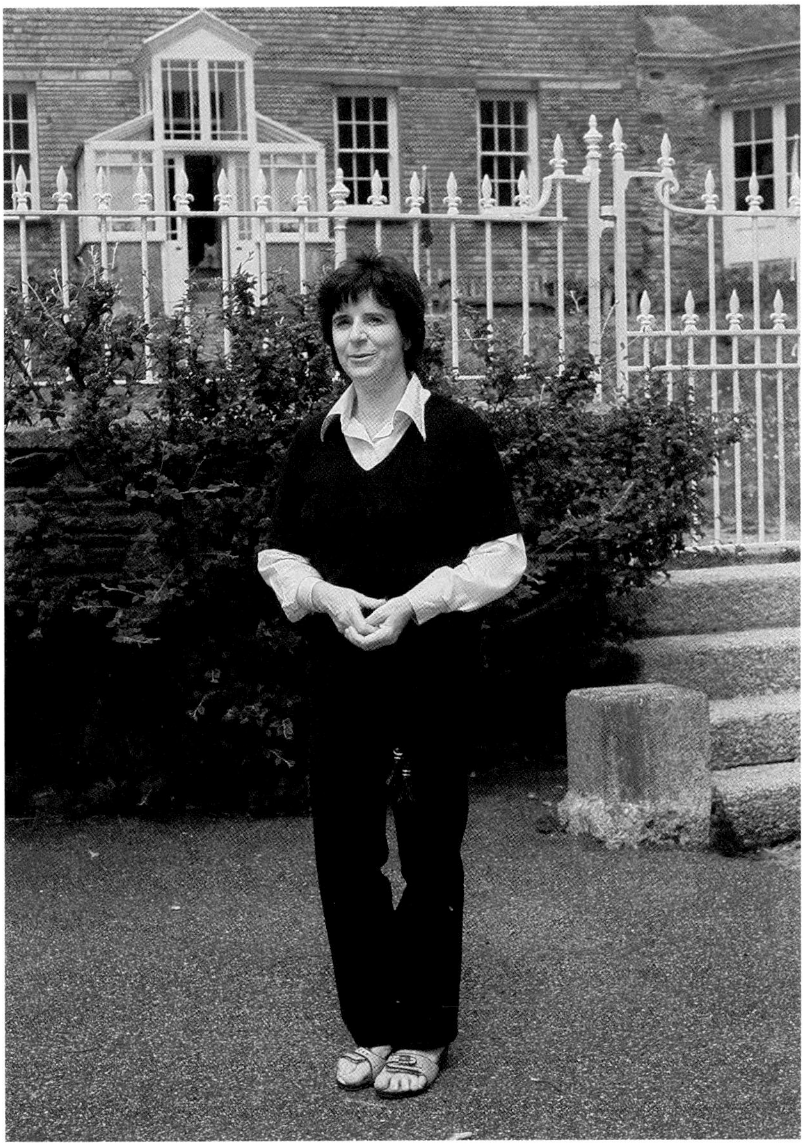

"They used to hang men at Four Turnings in the old days. Not any more, though." These lines were the conclu-

The vivacious Mrs. Esther Rowe, secretary and companion of Daphne du Maurier.

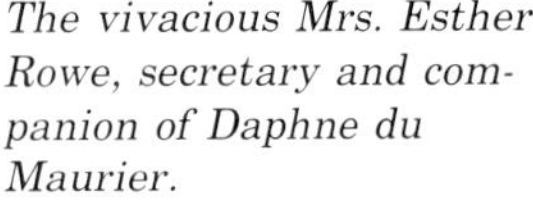

sion of her novel about Philip Ashley and his cousin Ambrose's wife, Rachel. Ambrose had died from a mysterious lingering malady at his wife's villa in Florence. Philip leaves England and goes to his cousin after receiving several accusing letters pertaining to his 'evil wife'. He arrives in Italy to find his beloved relative already dead and buried at Protestant Cemetery. Upon returning to Cornwall to the home he had once shared with his cousin, as manager of the estate, the thoughts of Rachel grow deeper and deeper with loathsomeness. How he hates her!

Philip's godfather recieves a letter saying that she had arrived in Plymouth with her late husband's effects—that Philip might like to have them. In spite of Philip's objections, he is persuaded to allow her to visit. Being only twenty-five and vulnerable, and she—an older beauty with the deceptive charm of a cobra, he completely falls under her spell. So against the advice of interested friends of his family he signs over to her the deeds to the house, the family jewels, and the entire estate under the mistaken idea that she would marry him. After joining into her nightly custom of a cup of tisana tea, he develops an illness identical to his wasted cousin. The poor fool! He finally recuperates from a five-week's illness and discovers the *real* Rachel...her coldness and overpowering lust for money.

With her great talent for horticulture and knowledge of herbs—she decided to relandscape the grounds. An enormous sunken garden is in construction and the overhead bridge was roughed in—merely framework. The foreman pulls Philip aside to warn him that if he went onto the terrace walk, not to stand on the bridgeway—"it doesn't bear any weight upon it. Anyone stepping onto it could fall and break his neck."

But Philip had so much on his mind . . . and they were all dressed and awaiting him for church. After the Sunday sermon the vicar, mopping his sweaty brow, asks Rachel how they combatted the heat in Italy. She describes her villa with the lovely patio cooled by a fountain and the overhanging laburnum tree. At the mention of 'laburnum' it all becomes clear to Philip; he remembers the villa's caretaker carefully sweeping up the fallen pods into a vessel . . . then the letter that had arrived containing the meaningless little seed — (the envelope that he had surreptitiously opened). Only recently live stock had been poisoned by the fallings of this death-bearing tree in the pasture close by. Domestically the pods could be crushed in the palms and placed undetected in tea or such.

Upon arriving home from church all dine together and afterwards Rachel requests companionship for a stroll to inspect the landscaping progress. All decline, so she ventures out alone . . . An hour passes—she deliberately was not warned of the dangerous condition of the garden structure.

Near the stones, mortar, and lumber above the sunken earth the two dogs stand whining. When Philip approaches he sees the dainty fresh footprints. Part of the bridge still remained dangling in the air . . . like a swinging ladder. He climbed down to the crumpled body. She looked up at him in pain . . . and there she died, uttering Ambrose's name.

" . . . they used to hang men at Four Turnings in the old days. Not any more, though".

. . . .

Perhaps the best known of all operas is Richard Wagner's *Tristan and Isolde* . . . if not for its plot, certainly for its music. The story that Wagner based his production on was a romance by Gottfried of Strassburg, telling the story of conflict between two lovers in medieval times on the shores of Cornwall. I don't believe Wagner was ever where I am standing, near the road of the Four Turnings, though. The gist of the tale is that King Mark of Cornwall sends Tristan (some say he was his son—others his nephew) to Ireland to bring back Isolde with whom he had fallen in love just from the glowing accounts of her. On being conducted to King Mark's fortress at Castle Dor she has already become enamoured with Tristan, who does nothing to encourage her. He treats her with courtesy, but does not permit himself to fall under her charm. Isolde becomes angry at his stoicism and orders her servant to brew a portion of poison. Tristan's appearance is requested and he goes to her. She asks him to drink a toast. He does so with indifference—she takes the cup to her lips expecting to die with him rather than marry the King. But it wasn't the deadly drink, it was a love potion instead that Brangaene, her companion, had prepared. The two look into each other's eyes with mutual passion.

"They used to hang men at Four Turnings in the old days. Not any more, though." These are the closing lines of <u>My Cousin Rachel,</u> by du Maurier. At this road intersection there is a monument — a very old stone bearing an inscription: "Tristan lies here, son of Mark." This seven foot roundish monolith was erected in the fifth century A.D. at Kilmarth ('Retreat of Mark'), but was moved to its present site by a preservation society.

134

They continue to Castle Dor, but are trapped in an intimate situation by a malicious knight, Melot. The King confronts the guilty pair and Tristan is overwhelmed with shame. An insult flies from the lips of Melot, and Tristan draws his sword, only to fall wounded. King Mark allows him to depart to a lonely half-ruined castle on the coast of Britanny. Isolde, also skilled in herbs and magic potions, tries to reach him to heal his wound, but he lives only long enough to die in her arms.

In the end King Mark learns of Brangaene's aphrodisiac mixture and feels great remorse for having separated the two lovers.

There are many variations of the romance. Historians and archaeologists say Tristan died in Cornwall—here, near the Four Turnings. We read the ancient inscription, "Drustans Hic Iacit—Cunomori Filius." I remembered enough of 'required' Latin to know that Filius was *son*, Drustans was *Tristan*, Hic—*here*. Shux! Why burst my brain when here's the translation lower on the pillar: Tristan lies here, son of Mark." This seven foot roundish monument was erected in the fifth century, A.D.— where stands a house (above an old foundation) that bears the name Kilmarth, which in Cornish means 'Retreat of Mark'. Its geography puts it correctly here, as the old language translates that the Cornish King Mark retreated to his home in his older years, where he could look out in peace across the open sea. This was Daphne du Maurier's present home.

The road by the monument will take us to Fowey. When we get to the Lanteglos highway we are nearing the Bodinnick ferry and will cross the estuary for 'Troy Town', as Sir Arthur Quiller Couch calls it in his stories of Cornwall. From the ferry we could see Swiss Cottage where Daphne du Maurier's sister now lives. Here the writer had spent much time before her marriage. We drove on to Fowey, parked the car outside of the city and walked to Frenchman's Creek Inn for tea. There were the tall chimneys and towers of Place House, which we had anticipated seeing—not just from the outside, but inside. We looked for an entrance way, but with no success decided to go to the real estate manager's office and inquire. The young lady in charge was most talented at repelling would-be visitors. I tried every crafty wile in my voluble repertoire, but she had learned her lines

well, "very sorry, it's strictly private property. No, you cannot call them for permission to enter. Yes, Mrs. Treffry still lives there. They've been in residency for five hundred years. Good day." Our first failure. Well, I'll write to the owner when I return to the States. No Englishman fails to respond to a letter.

If you are a good walker you will love Fowey. But it's too late in the day for us to start hiking along the coast. The Trust owns most of the coastline from the Gribbin (close to Fowey) on for the next eight miles east.

St. Catherine's Castle, a fort built by Henry VIII, stands above the harbour mouth of Fowey. It was constructed to protect the fast growing trade in shipping that was developing here. The history of this little seaport is fascinating; in the French Wars of the fourteenth and fifteenth centuries its ships were the most advanced in the English fleet. The eight miles, eastward, between Polruan and Polperro are delightful. Here the cliffs are high, but the land is calm and friendly, punctuated with the church spires of Lanteglos and Lansallos. You could spread your lunch on the mossy turf and afterwards lie back and watch the fluffy white puffs of clouds chasing one another across a field of pale blue sky. As a child I always thought of the upper space as being God's domain—and I guess I still do. That must account for my repugnance at the thought of mechanical bodies invading the heavenly regions. The stratosphere just isn't equipped with the necessities of man—. Yes, as some would declare, He *allowed* the human to achieve things that seemed impossible, as He didn't tie him down—but I feel sure a Pandora's box was opened. Oh well, this is certainly no place to fret about man's meddling: I must absorb all that's about me—the simple wild orchid that my weight has crushed—and there is the tiny pinkblossom called Centaury (I know its name because I looked through Mrs. Young's wild flower book at the farm).

More Cornwall Villages

Dick says it's too late now to go to Port Eliot or Antony House. So that's on for tomorrow.

When the Flemish sculptor John Rysbrack (born 1693 in the lower countries) came to England, the first piece he was commissioned to do (age 29) was a monument to Edward Eliot in St. Germans church, a stone-throw from Port Eliot. The Eliots, Earls of St. Germans, had a large elegant manor that can be seen from the churchyard.

St. Germans is one of the most winsome villages in Cornwall. To the east, a short distance from the town, is a lovely quay which is no longer used commercially, but creates a fine pastoral scene with a high raised viaduct spanning it; ducks and swans were converging on the banks of the water. To the west of the village is a row of interesting seventeenth century almshouses. Peace reigned supreme the day we visited the splendid little church. King Athelstan, in 936, established a bishopric here for Devon and Cornwall, but in the mid-eleventh century it was moved to Crediton. Twenty years later a priory of Augustinian monks moved in the vacated house and it became the church we now see. On the west front is the marvelous cathedral-like door, flanked on both sides by towers in differing style. The lower parts of the towers are Norman structure, with the spire to the north built in the early twelve hundreds, and the south one in the fourteen hundreds. It is truly a palimpsest building . . . each era and its restoration done in good taste. The great east window is by Burne-Jones and the colouring is exquisite.

There is a medieval misericord left from the original abbey choir that commemorates the legend of Dando. It is a carving of Dando the hunter with his dog. On his shoulders is slung his cross-bow and his game hanging on the stock of his weapon. This hunter was a monk of St. Germans Priory who was unfaithful to his vows. His companions were ones who enjoyed the 'good things of life'. His fame became widespread, and his appetite for the game-chase was insatiable. When not gaming he was drinking the fruit of the vine.

While hunting one morning near St. Germans his wine gave out before his thirst was quenched and he called for more. Told that there *was* no more he cried out that they could "get it from Hell". Suddenly a stranger rode up midst them and offered Dando his flask, which the monk emptied hastily. The hunter was immediately transformed into a terrible fiend and began fighting with the visitor over the cap-

The Eliots, Earls of St. Germans, had a large elegant manor that can be seen from the road. St. Germans is one of the most winsome villages in Cornwall. King Athelstan established a bishopric here in 936 that connects the property to Port Eliot.

tured game. When Dando fell from his horse the stranger jumped into Dando's saddle and dragged the poor monk away with him. The horse was terrified and broke into a wild gallop, plunging them into the dank waters of the River Lynher. That was the end of the pair and beast.

Dando's companions changed their lives. They began to devote themselves to the service of God and His Church, making rich gifts to the Priory as thank offerings for their deliverance from the fate of Dando.

A few miles away was Antony House. In 1602 Richard Carew wrote his famous *Survey of Cornwall*, a valuable document used in the present times for information. For over five hundred years the Carews have lived in Antony House, about a mile from the Torpoint ferry. Cornish history is more closely associated with the great Antony House than any other in the West Country. Richard Carew watched the Armada move up the coast and reported the raid on the town of Newlyn. The family did not have an easy time of it during the Civil Wars that followed in his grandson's days. Sir Alexander Carew was the most tragic figure of that period. First he supported Parliament at the despair of his family, who even hid all his portraits for the shame of it. Later on he began to have doubts about the rightness of the Roundheads (the Cromwellians), but it was his undoing, as his disloyalty was guessed and he was executed in 1644. His brother, John Carew, sixteen years afterwards suffered a similar fate at the restoration.

In years to follow, the grandson of Sir Alexander Carew, who was a fervent Stuart supporter, was put under preventive arrest, but his home, Antony, was not completed until 1721. The estate passed through the female line to the Reginald Poles. They, in turn, enlarged and improved the parks and gardens. All through the nineteenth century the owners were active in the affairs of East Cornwall in the House of Parliament. In 1961 Antony House was given to the National Trust.

A forecourt of arcaded pavilions gives entrance to the silverish gray Pentewan stone of Antony House. To James Gibbs, whose name is connected with the building care of such as Radcliffe Camera at Oxford and St. Martin-in-the-Fields in London, goes much credit for its beauty, though the original architect of Antony is unknown.

140

Inside there is rare panelling in Dutch oak and the rooms contain good accessories: pieces of English Renaissance furniture, paintings that illustrate the history of Cornwall, family portraits, and excellent china. Incidentally, poor Sir Alexander Carew was restored to an honoured position after he was considered a martyr in the eyes of the Royalists. There is also a first edition of *The Survey of Cornwall* on display opened to these lines:

"In the 1588's Richard Carew lived through Antony's most alarming and dangerous period. Spanish raiding parties ravaged the countryside, and the progress of the Armada was watched coming up the coast of Cornwall." These were days when few noblemen lived in this remote land—separated from the rest of England by the River Tamar. Richard went up to Oxford at age eleven to become a 'gentleman commonor' of Christ Chruch; but instead of going abroad afterwards, as most did, he was admitted to Middle Temple then returned to take up his responsibilities. He became the most respected Cornishman of his time. He died at his prayers in 1620 and was buried in the church at Antony.

The long way back to the farm will put us on the moors after dark sets in—that's alright, a new chain of short-order-

141

meals has opened up called The Little Chef. We found the food good and the service very satisfactory. Tomorrow we would retrace our steps as far as Plympton, near Plymouth, to visit Saltram, a beautiful Devon manor.

The day was perfect . . . the dew still glistened on the dark velvet green of the conifers against a soft blue sky; we headed almost straight south over the moors to Buckfastleigh, the home of the Grenvilles at one time and the Drakes at another. Then a short drive from there would take us to Saltram. In the fifteen and sixteen hundreds the manor belonged to the Bagg family, but passed on to the Caterets in the 1660's. Fifty years later a local squire, George Parker, bought it and the Parkers remained there until The National Trust acquired it in 1957. It became a memorial to those who died in the Second World War.

Inside there remain Tudor and Stuart contributions of its earlier owners, but it was the Parkers who employed Robert Adam to build the present building around the original construction. There were also extensive alterations made to the east wing in 1768, and the Library was added

to the southwest corner. A decade later the entrance porch was attached.

Since country homes, in their heyday, were lived in only a short time of the year, they were kept shuttered the rest of the while, and furniture was covered. Nowadays the fine manors are receiving more wear in one season than they formerly did in a decade. So one must bear with the poor lighting and prohibition of sophisticated camera equipment. One dear hostess, who observed our despair in attempts to get any photos, accommodated us by opening the Holland blinds.

As you enter the Entrance Hall there are two dominating portraits: one is of the 'proud and willful owner' Lady Catherine Parker, and the other of her son. Note the chimneypiece—it relates in carving the story of Androcles and the Lion. There were Chinese procelain dishes of the Ch'ien Lung reign (1736-95) on the table. When the first Parker became Earl of Morley the mahogany hall chairs were painted with the Earl's arms to memorialize that honour.

In the Morning Room, which I thought the loveliest part of the house, the walls were covered with Genoa silk velvet and they, in turn, covered with pictures almost touching each other. Sir Joshua Reynolds, a frequent visitor in the house and had been born in the neighbouring parish of Plympton St. Maurice, had helped in the selections of portraits and landscapes chosen. Five of them were done by Reynolds, himself—and the portrait over the mantle of John Parker III and his sister, Theresa, he declared the best composition he had ever done. The room contains many fine objects of art: Chinese *famille* rose punch bowls, black basalte lamps by Wedgewood, Chippendale cabinets on stands, and Adams serpentine-shaped tables.

In the Velvet Drawing Room almost everything dates from the period of George II. To the left of the fireplace is a Louis XIV writing desk in brass and tortoiseshell that is considered very valuable. The pictures in this room are mainly Flemish and Dutch with four views of Naples by Gabrielle Riccardelli (1741-77).

The Saloon is magnificent; two floors were made into one to form a "double cube" of fifty feet long by twenty-five feet wide and twenty-five feet high.

In the Dining Room the Axminster carpet was woven

to match the pattern of the ceiling above. Then in the Staircase Hall we found another large writing desk that King Louis XIV had given Sarah, Duchess of Marlborough, who later gave it to her granddaughter Lady Catherine Parker. It is completely covered in marquetry of tortoiseshell, coloured inlays of mother-of-pearl, ivory and painted woods.

When you visit there, don't fail to see the upstairs Chinese wallpapers, also look for the carved Spanish proverb . . . "Take what you want, says God. Take it, and pay for it." . . . showing a bear robbing a hive of bees.

It took all afternoon to visit all the bedrooms. After that there was still to be seen the Mirror Room, the Garden and the Garden Room. A door in the outer wall leads you to the Chapel, the Orangery, the Castle and the Great Kitchen. In the Tudor Court refreshments can be had. (Oh, my poor feet!)

After a good night's sleep we would go to Bovey Tracy; there would be much to see in the surrounding countryside. First, we'd stop at Drogo Castle at Drewsteignton near Chagford one mile south of the A30.

At the closing of the nineteenth century, architecture was taking on a different expression. The agricultural depression had completed the evolution from a 'landed gentry' to an industrial social and financial scene. Earlier the nation was dominated by an aristocracy of wealth *and* land—but now the frame had shrunk . . . there were more rich people . . . less room to turn in. A female Minister of the Labour Party gleefully announced: "We don't cut off their heads anymore we just shrink their horizons!" . . . referring to the old aristocracy.

Castle Drogo in Devon is an example of this, built by Sir Edwin Lutyens, dating from 1910. I do not admire its architectural anachronisms. The wedging of flint rock into the mortar between the granite stones (reminiscent of Queen Isabella's castle at Segovia, Spain, 1500's), Norman columns in the interior, and its flat silhouette—like the ruined Ragland—render the castle ineffectual in force and conviction. But then, it will be a link in the continuity of the history of house-building.

It was built for Julius Drewe who in the late nineteenth century launched 'The Home and Colonial Stores'. The architect Lutyens had previously transformed the small

Saltram's interior is magnificent. The Morning Room I thought the lovliest, with its walls covered in Genoa silk velvet and they, in turn, covered with pictures almost touching each other. Sir Joshua Reynolds, a frequent visitor in the house, considered the portrait over the mantle of young John Parker III and his sister the finest work he had ever done.

145

medieval fortress of Lindesfarne Castle on Holy Island in a masterful creation of calculated asymmetry.

Drogo is probably the last castle or private house of that size that will be built in England.

From here we would reach Lustleigh just in time for our noon invitation to lunch with the Craddocks—a relative of our friend Phil Davis of Birmingham. We had known Jean Craddock's family for fifteen years. Much had happened to them since her husband had died at their home in Shepton Mallet, where he was a shoe manufacturer. They sold the business to the Clark Shoe Factory . . . a name that was glaring from the front pages of all the sensational newspapers. "Clark heiress found dead in swimming pool at Dartington Hall Arts Institute. Miss Clark was known to be a good swimmer." Dartington Hall was only ten miles from Lustleigh . . . as the crow flies.

Our host's home was situated on an outcrop of land that overlooked Cleaves Valley. The beauty was too fantastic for me to take in. I could think only of the Creator who provided it all; most call it *Nature*, but *she* is just His servant.

> "Nature great parent! whose unceasing hand
> Rolls round the seasons of the changeful year
> How mighty, how majestic are thy works!
> With what a pleasing dread they swell the soul,
> That sees astonished, and astonished sings!"*

I could not bear to live here for fear of becoming sated to the extent of taking all this scenery for granted. But when I leave I can carry the picture in my heart. For miles and miles my eyes could scan trees of every shade of green, declivities where brooks babbled over the broken stones and burst into sparkling foam. Then Dick brought me out of my reverie . . . and we said our goodbyes with regret at leaving such a garden of Eden.

Two miles NW of Totnes we reached Dartington Hall—then backtracked to Totnes. Dartington Hall was a beautiful place situated on the River Dart. A modern experimental institute had been built on the ancient thirteenth century estate. The Hall was still standing on the grounds but was roofless. Summer plays and musicals were performed in the evenings. And here was the dammed-up part of

146

the river where all the excitement took place about the
drowned Clark heiress.

This was the day for the medieval fair at Totnes. Every
Tuesday the ladies of the town dress in Elizabethan costumes
and do their shopping and gossip with the visitors. We were
having so much fun with photographing them all that we
forgot about going to Bovey Tracy . . . but perhaps tomorrow.

*James Thomson (1727)

*For miles and miles my
eye could see trees of
every shade of green and
little declivities where
brooks babbled over
broken stones and burst
into sparkling foam.*

WHITBREAD
KING WILLIAM IV
TO LET

Back to Devon

The next morning an article in the Daily Express brought on a great desire to visit the castle at Ugbrooke, in South Devon. The item began with the explanation of one of Britain's tax laws—and one that was new to me: *death duties.* It ran on that Lord Clifford of Chudleigh and his wife faced exile in an humble cottage in Guernsey. The Earl was advised by his finance counselor that the *death duties* would ruin his family and break up his estate. His 3000 acre country place would have to be sold to raise the approximate sum of 1,500,000 pounds that would be due the Crown (The pound has fluctuated over the last twenty years from $2.70 a pound to as low as $1.14). The motto of Lord Clifford's home was "Semper Paratus" (Always Ready), "and though", he was quoted, "I am heart-broken at the thought of leaving, if that is the only solution . . ."

The Earl's decision was that he and his wife put Ugbrooke House into a trust for their eldest son and they themselves would depart for the three-bedroom stone cottage on an island off the coast of the English Channel between England and France.

In 1956 Lord Clifford inherited the estate, but it was in a ruinous condition. Over the thirty years he had bought back many priceless treasures of the former owner-kinsmen who had sacrificed them to the auctioneer. He lovingly restored all damaged parts, and redecorated the house. In 1980 the lower part was opened to the public. To quote Lord Clifford: "The last thing on earth I want to do is move from the place I consider I have saved. And, financially, I shall be much worse off. So no snide remarks about a tax haven, please."

So off to Nr. Chudleigh, heading south on the A380 (the Exeter-Torbay road) to the ancestral home of Lord Clifford. As we reached the turn-off for the estate, we were overwhelmed by the size of the trees. I do not exaggerate when I say that a hundred cars could be parked under the branches

We visited Totnes on the day for the medieval fair. Every Tuesday, in the summer months, the ladies of the town dress in Elizabethan costumes and do their shopping and gossip with each other.

149

of each great elm. We paid the one pound and twenty pence
and would be free to roam the three thousand acres of natural
beauty for the rest of the day. Chudleigh is on the River
Teign and a tributary of it runs through the Castle grounds.
There, on the bank were three small row boats for the
pleasure of guests. Close by is Chudleigh Rock, a picturesque site, commanding a fine view and containing two caves.
You will also see Syon Abbey, the only surviving Pre-
Reformation house, built in 1420. The Castle Chapel was
open, but the rest of the estate was closed on Fridays . . .and
that was today.

Ugbrooke was not the only manor looking for a tenant;
when we visited Lord Courtenay at Powderham Castle, near
Exeter, he related the same plight about his ancestral home.
It seems that no *one* family can stand the financial drain
of the cost of upkeep; they hoped they would be able to stay
on in the wing used as living quarters. "Neither of us wants
to leave, but if we have to go, to ensure the future of the
Castle, then we will", Lady Courtenay (Devon) declared. The
Castle attracts thousands of paying sightseers every year, but
Powderham is still taking a thumping loss. It costs at least
25,000 pounds a year to run, and this year an overall loss
of 15,000 pounds or more is expected. The castle is being
subsidized by the rest of the estate being run as an agricultural
unit by Lord Courtenay—and if present trends continue it
will lead to bankruptcy. So Powderham is up for lease.
Anybody for a nice big house . . . good for a hotel, flats, or
headquarters for a large company?

Chudleigh was Church land from the earliest times,
which included Ugbrooke Hall, the house of the Precentor
to the Bishop of Exeter. The ruins of the Bishop's summer
Palace can still be seen. The property of the house was mentioned as early as 1080, and remained the Precentor's until
the defeat of the Western Rebellion of 1549. Then the Duke
of Somerset, Lord Protector, took Ugbrooke for himself and
dissolved the Church ownership of the Chudleigh lands. On
the site, in the beginning of Tudor times, an E-shaped manor
had been built around an ancient earlier building. The Duke
of Somerset held Ugbrooke for only ten years and sold it to
Sir Piers Courtenay of Powderham, at Exeter. Sir Piers had
no son, so Ugbrooke passed to their daughter who married
Anthony Clifford, Squire of Kingsteignton in Devonshire

One can spend an entire day roaming the grounds of Ugbrooke House with its lake, great elms and church. Lord Clifford inherited the estate in 1956 when it was in ruinous condition. He lovingly restored all damaged parts and bought back precious ornaments that had previously been auctioned.

151

A portrait of the First Lord Clifford of Ugbrooke House.

and Borscombe in Wiltshire. The house remained a Tudor Manor until 1750, then the fourth Lord Clifford commissioned Robert Adam to remodel the place, and 'Capability' Brown to design the park. It was Adam who added the castellated towers, planned the main rooms, library and chapel. Brown dammed up the Ugbrooke River to create three lakes in the surrounding park.

The Cliffords are descendants of Robert, third Duke of Normandy, who came to England with William the Conqueror. Walter Clifford was the father of 'Fair Rosamond', the famed romantic mistress of Henry II. Someone wrote:

> "Queen Eleanor reckoned
> That Harry the Second
> Should have shunned
> Fair Rosamond
> Therein they differed
> About Miss Clifford"

The long illustrious credentials of the Clifford family could fill volumes of books. They were prominent in the fields of the military as generals, the Church as Bishops, and one in the scientific world as an authority on light rays.

Our alloted days in Wessex were running out, so we would devour all we could of this Eden. I really couldn't bear the thought of leaving Cornwall without seeing Trerice. In reading Daphne du Maurier's *The King's General*, Sir John Arundell (the builder of Trerice), was one of the supporters of the Royalist's cause. Prior to the Civil War of the 1640's he had served as a soldier in the low countries, which may have influenced his choice of 'Dutch gables' with their typical scrolled finials, for they are not found anywhere else in the West Country at such an early date as 1573.

To get there we'd drive west through Okehampton, then skirt along Bridestowe to Lifton, Launceston, and a stop at Altarnun on Bodmin Moor for our lunch. We hadn't been there for more than ten minutes before we were invited to tea with some townspeople that we had fallen into conversation with. This was a favourite village of mine, anyway, since reading *Jamaica Inn* . . . about the albino vicar that was leader of a smuggling gang. There are many ancient earthworks and standing stones on Bodmin Moors. We are so close to Dozmary Pool that it's hard not to take a side road and revisit those waters where "an arm clothed in white samite rose to catch Excalibur and draw him under in the mere". But we have distance to cover, so on past Rough Tor to Bodmin, the capital (with Truro) of Cornwall. Bodmin holds the distinction of having the largest medieval church (1400's) in Cornwall.

Since reading Jamaica Inn I had longed to see the place. On a bleak day it can look as spooky as Daphne du Maurier describes it. It stands all alone on Bodmin Moor with Dosmary Pool being the closest landmark. (Dosmary Pool was where Sir Bedevere was ordered by King Arthur to throw Excalibur.)

From here we drove to St. Colum-Major with it's lovely Decorated Perpendicular church (dedicated to a maiden, St. Columba)—with a moated vicar's rectory. The lofty earthworks of Castle-an-Dinas, which local people connect with King Arthur lies about two miles southeast of here. At. St. Columb we take the A3059 for Crantock, very close to Newquay. It was a gray town with hundreds and hundreds of boarding houses inhabited by very bored visitors looking for something to do. That isn't the way the guide books read, though. They paint it as a seaside and golfing resort with excellent accommodations, lying on a picturesque coast. But there are excursions from there that are inviting. One is six miles north to the charming village of St. Mawgan-in-Pydar. The church dates from the twelve hundreds with good brasses and wood carvings. Now by descending west through the

154

Vale of Lanherne you find the manor house of the Arundells that is now turned into a Carmalite nunnery. (That was a switch—in most cases it's the nunnery that was turned into a manor house). A short distance southwest of here is Trerice.

The tall Cornish hedges bordering the driveway led to the manor of Trerice. This also had belonged to the Arundells, one of the two families of the most distinguished Cornish gentry . . . the other being the Grenvilles of Stowe. Both have passed out of existence now. But here was a quiet, peaceful spot with the little river Gannel running through the grounds down to the sandy beach. Very little change has taken place in over five hundred years. Inside the manor is the Great Hall, lit by tremendous windows of twenty-four lights each, with a beautifully ornamented ceiling of plastered strapwork (decoration of bands interlaced with each other similar to fretwork or cut leather), medallions and pendents. This style prevailed in the Netherlands in the 1540's. The fireplace mantle is supported by caryatids holding a scroll dated 1572. (I had seen one other such at Collocombe, in Devon, the home of Edmund Tremayne, bearing the date 1574—and behind the wall a secret door opened into what was called a "priest's hole"—a place to hide the catholic priest after the Reformation in England). At the top of the stairs at Trerice was a solar with a huge semicircular bay window that flooded the room with light from the south.

There are no craftsmen today that would attempt to do the intricate stuccowork that is the main feature of Trerice, Collocombe, and Buckland Abbey. That is why I am so angered at modern art—some persons with exalted delusions think they are justified in living the Bohemian life because they sling a little paint, and entitle their canvas "Guess What"! Forgive me, dear reader (if I *have* one left) . . . that just popped out.

We have several hours of daylight left so let's return to the farm by the north coast of Cornwall until we reach Bude, then cut across into Devon on the A3072 as far as Hatherleigh. Dropping a few miles south we'll be on the A30 at Okehampton just five miles east of Sticklepath.

Wadebridge, a town on the Camel estuary, is redeemed from dullness only by the fine old fifteen-arch bridge dating from the 1480's which is considered the most ancient main road bridge in every-day-usage in Britian. It was paid for by the sale of wool. One of the oldest railways in England (1834) connects Wadebridge with Bodmin.

On the Port Issac coastal road, perched on the cliff edge, is a folly called Doyden Castle, built in 1830. Before reaching Tintagel you will find slate quarries, in fact one of the largest man-made holes on earth. This is Delabole. Eden Phillpotts, the colorful descriptive writer of the West Country, called it 'St. Tid' in his narratives.

Next is the most well-known site in England. The very name of Tintagel rings with magic. Here on the promontory are ruins of King Arthur's birthplace.

> " . . . . and on the night
> When Uther in Tintagil past away
> Moaning and wailing for an heir, . . ."
> "It seem'd in heaven, a ship like
> A dragon wing'd, and all from stern to stern"
> Was seen. And those viewing say
> "The great sea fall, wave after wave,
> Each mightier than the last
> Til last a ninth one, gathering half the deep" . . .
> "Slowly rose and plunged wildly, and the flames
> Were on fire, when down the wave was borne
> A naked babe and deposited at Merlin's feet,
> Who stooped and caught the babe, and cried,
> 'The King! Here is an heir for Uther'".

(Excerps from Tennyson)

The castle, before becoming ruins, was used by the Earls of Cornwall as a stronghold. This is beautiful wild scenery, such as you'll not find an equal anywhere on earth. On the cliffs west of the village is S.S. Materiana and Marcelliana Parish Church which contains some traces of Saxon work and a Norman arch. From here to Boscastle is an area for hiking with paths leading to waterfalls and pretty look-outs. If onlyTintagel could be separated from the tourists—how wonderful it would be.

Boscatle is the most curious of all the English harbours. Ships know better than to enter it at any time but when the seas are calm—it can be terrifying at any other. The present curved jetty was built by Sir Richard Grenville in 1584 and except for a slight reconditioning it is as good as it was four hundred years ago. This was our first return visit since 1970, which I can distinctly remember as being the coldest I ever was in my life . . . and it being July!

There is a marvelous sight if you go beyond the outer breakwater to the 'blowing hole'. When the tide rises and causes the water to thump through the hole, a sudden spurt of spume is thrown over the harbour entrance. What a thing to watch!

Soon Crackington comes into view. The architecture of the buildings is not attractive, but the coastline is good; the rocky cliffs and projecting abutments out into the Atlantic were charming to the Victorian romantics. Tennyson was lavish in his descriptions. Not too far away is the terrible Strangles, a beach leading up to a height of 731 ft—highest in Cornwall—a scene of dramatic action in Thomas Hardy's *A Pair of Blue Eyes*.

From Chipman Point to the Lizzard is a mile of the wildest cliffs. The Duchy of Cornwall gave this stretch of coastline, along with many many other miles, to the National Trust. We head straight on along Sandymouth until we come to Bude.

Bude is a favourite summer and golfing resort with a mild climate and beautiful coast scenery. The road we take is eastward to Stratton, about one and a half miles. There is a fine Perpendicular church, Launcells, that contains the tomb of Sir John Arundell (1561). Close by is Stamford Hill, where, in 1643, the Parliamentarians were defeated by Sir Richard Grenville and the Cornish army. The A3072 goes to Hatherleigh. At Hatherleigh we follow the A386 almost straight south to Okehampton where we arrived just in time for supper at the Post Boy Restaurant. Five miles east takes us to our farm-haven and we are ready for a good night's rest!

Our last day in Devon would be spent in a visit to our old friends in Minehead, in Somersetshire. Muriel Bullivant was recovering bravely from her husband Cecil's death. John, their son, and Babs (his wife) were there. Babs had baked sesame seed cake, and there was Devon cream with strawberries, thinly sliced fresh bread spread with butter, homemade jams and pots of tea. Our visit over and goodbys tearfully exchanged, we left for Bideford and Great Torrington, crossing Exmoor National Park just south of the Doone

Valley—hideout of the Doone outlaw gang in Blackmore's novel *Lorna Doone*. We stopped briefly at Simonsbath, so named from a pool in the Barle above the bridge. If we were younger we'd cut north a bit toward Challacombe to see Shoulsbarrow Castle, an Iron Age Fort, but it's after five o'clock so must hurry on. Bideford (Biddyford), a small and ancient seaport, is situated picturesquely between two hills rising on the side of the Torridge River that is spanned by a beautiful bridge of twenty-four arches, originally erected in the fourteenth century. The church here is re-built but keeps the Norman front. A Red Indian was brought home by Sir Richard Grenville (an uncle of another Richard Grenville) and baptized here under the name of Christian Rawley in 1588, the first Indian ever seen in England.

The town is closely associated with Charles Kingsley's *Westward Ho!*, written for the most part here in Bideford. Facing the quay is a tall statue of Kingsley (1819-1875). From here to Torrington is five miles. Torrington is a small town with scanty remains of a castle from the Edwardian days. This was where Lord Fairfax defeated the Royalists in 1646. Three miles northward is Wear Giffard Mansion of the fourteen hundreds—it has a hall with a magnificent, carved oaken roof.

Now, by winding in and out of high bordering hedges we just watch the sun and follow our noses south to Okehampton and to our last night's lodging at Forde Farm. Parting was painful next morning, but we made it with the firm promise of being back the following summer. We never got back . . . but I will always remember Devon and when bleak times come my heart will be warmed by my memories. Perhaps I will get to tell you why I was exiled from this Eden before I lay down my pen for the last time.

But back to 1984. We scurried on toward Dorset, to Bournemouth. I have written at great lengths about the charms of this Channel resort, the favourite of many notables: Disraeli, Queen Victoria, Sir Walter Scott, Robert Louis Stevenson, Winston Churchill and countless others, in *Dorset Forever* and *Return to Wessex*. Bournemouth has a wonderful beach, boasts of two Symphony Orchestras, is a sporting center, and has a quantity of Museums. Thomas Hardy, in *Tess of the D'Urbervilles*, identifies Bournemouth with Sandbourne where the murder tragedy of the story takes

place. Its closeness to the New Forest, Salisbury, Winchester, Wimborne, Weymouth, Milton Abbey, Romsey and many other thrilling places makes it doubly attractive.

We would be here two weeks and visit all our old trysting spots and ghostly haunts. It seemed I had a vigil to keep in the heart of Wessex. After greeting the hosts, Powells and Reasts, we unpacked the luggage in our old room that we'd occupied so many times.

Someone Who Knew Thomas Hardy

Tomorrow Dorchester would be top on the list. It was only twenty-five miles away to the west. I was in the mood for Thomas Hardy . . . could feel my old love for his poetry and novels taking over my affections. First off, after reaching the little city we took lunch at The Olde Tea Shop (1600), and later went to Stinsford Church, the setting of *Under the Greenwood Tree*, first published in 1872, a story of the Mellstock Quire (choir) and its serious 'west-gallery musicians' . . . its pages all peppered with crusty old characters of the 1850's. It is one of the few books written by Hardy that was not a tragic one. Really a delightful little novel it is, written about all that was so much a part of his environment at Upper Mellstock (the village of Higher Bockhampton) two miles northeast of Dorchester.

There under the beautiful old trees we paused at the grave of Dorchester's greatest writer—whose everyday prose sounded like poetry. While we gaped at the tomb, an elderly man hobbled to our side, having just come from the church service, and inquired if he might help us. He introduced himself as Mr. Chiles, and seeing our absorption in the inscription on the tomb told us that he, himself, was only a boy of fourteen in 1910 when he first became aware of Mr. Hardy in the church choir, still singing at the age of seventy. He related many youthful experiences and antics about

Informal garden at Bournemouth, a resort city on the English Channel.

161

him as a local character. I could hardly believe that I was talking with a person who had sung side by side with Thomas Hardy, the novelist born in 1840, close to the old church of Stinsford. Of course we were invited to tea . . . that inevitably follows in a case like this. We couldn't accept, as our plans were to go to Wolfeton (in earlier times spelled Wolveton) in this area.

But first we would see "Egdon Heath", the setting of Hardy's *The Return of the Native.* Nowhere on my map was such an area. On asking a native how to find it he laughed me to scorn, by saying, "no sech place, madam." Hardy had only taken certain geographical features of the general locale . . . scattered bits of remote margins of waste

While standing by the grave of Thomas Hardy an elderly man, like an apparition, touched my shoulder. "Might I be of some help?", he inquired. He introduced himself as Mr. Chiles . . . he had known Mr. Hardy when he was a young man. When Thomas Hardy was eighty he was still singing in the Stinsford choir; young Chiles was about fourteen and training with the singers. I felt privileged to meet a link between the great author and myself.

land. . . and brought them all together in a small section, as though it were one heath. In disappointment we went looking for Maumbury Rings (218 feet long, 163 feet wide) and had more success. It has long been considered the largest and most perfect amphitheatre in the country. The Romans had utilized it from an earlier existing civilization, as it was of pre-Roman date. There is another Roman camp, spelled Poundbury (but pronounced Pommery), close by. And two miles south of Dorchester is Maiden Castle, one of the finest prehistoric forts in England, covering one hundred and fifteen acres of Fordington Hill. Leaving the ancient military works we head N.W. to Wolveton.

In a quiet meadow west of Dorchester, near the junction of the tiny Cerne river and the Frome (Froom) we came across a treasure . . . The first indication of its importance was the massively built gatehouse with two round towers of unequal size and off-centered archway leading to the manor house. Above the archway was a cartouche displaying the arms of three great families: Mohuns, Jurdain, and Trenchards—but the Jurdains were new to me . . . newcomers, I guess.

The name Wolveton is of Saxon origin . . . then bells went off in my mind! Thomas Hardy wrote a book of short stories called "A Group of Noble Dames", and it was centered here in an ivy-covered manor house, its appearance much enhanced by the size of the numerous mullioned windows.

The tale of Lady Penelope was delightful, relating the situation of the clever Penelope in dealing with her three suitors courting her on the lawns of Wolveton. "You foolish men, have patience—in due time I will marry you all". A roguish, coy remark, made as a jest, was later fulfilled in reality.

But back to earlier times: there has been a dwelling place on the site since the 800's. The present manor was completed in 1495, according to a date on the gatehouse. Older parts of the house predate the 13th century.

This historic place is unknown to tourists as it has not been turned over to the National Trust. In 1480 Wolveton came to the Trenchards. (The first mention, to my knowledge, of the Trenchards was in the reign of Henry II. The manor of Lewtrenchard passed on from them, through

marriage, to the Monks of Potheridge, but in 1626 Thomas Monk fell into debt and an ancestor of S. Baring-Gould purchased the estate.) The Wolveton Trenchards had followed the owners, John Mohun, who had a daughter whose son was John Trenchard. Trenchard was sheriff of Dorset, and served many years as Commissioner of the Peace. His great grandson, George, was knighted by Queen Elizabeth I. He became Governor of Sandsfoot Castle that stands at Portland Isle, and during the Armada he was in charge of making inventory of the stores of captured Spanish ships.

The house at Wolveton became deserted and neglected from a time in the 1800's, and the property sold to the cousins Hennings of Dorchester. From there it went to the Westons who prevented it from falling into a derelict building. In 1874 the Kingston Lacy family came to live here and in the present time it has passed on to Captain Thimbleby—a connexion of the Mohuns and Trenchards.

Wolveton has had its spooky moments. There was the incident in 1640—a large company was seated in the dining hall. Around the walls of the room was a series of carved figures of the Kings of England. It is recorded that at this time (the third of November—the day the Long Parliament began to sit) during the lull of conversation the scepter fell

164

from the hand of King Charles I's effigy . . . an ill omen, indeed, foretelling the beheading of the king in 1649.

Then another: during the mid-sixteen hundreds an Assize Judge came to dine, but after being seated, he suddenly arose, ordered his carriage and left for home. On the way back to Dorchester he told the marshall that he had seen a vision of Lady Trenchard's figure standing behind her chair with her throat cut and her head dangling under her arm. A messenger soon overtook him on horseback to tell him the news that Lady Trenchard had committed suicide.

All hasn't been on the gloomy note, though. One of the family members won a very fine wager (early in the seventeen hundreds) when he reached the top of the Great Stairs at Wolveton in a horse and carriage. Many say the prank has been repeated numerous times by the driver's ghost.

Wolveton's handsomest piece is no longer to be seen in the Great Hall. In 1804 Queen Charlotte and George III made a visit here and admired a fine octagonal marble table supported by eight rampant lions. At such fervent admiring remarks the hostess felt obligated to present it to the queen, and it is now at Frogmore at Windsor Castle.

The event I like best that occurred at Wolveton concerns the surprise visit (a surprise to the guest and the hostess) made by Philip the Fair of Austria and his Spanish wife Joanna (or Juana la loca, as historical romance refers to her). Joanna was the daughter of Isabella and Ferdinand, and the heir of her father's Castile and her mother's Aragon. In January 1506, the royal couple were on their way from the Netherlands to claim the throne of Castile when a terrible storm on the English Channel made them take cover at Weymouth in Dorset. At this time Sir Thomas Trenchard was living at Wolveton and received news of the distressed ship. He gathered a small force of men to aid the foreign unidentified passengers. Being unable to understand their language, and they being ignorant of English, Sir Thomas sent for his learned young kinsman John Russell of Bridport to act as interpreter. Later, when Joanna and Philip were invited to visit Windsor Castle, Russell accompanied them and cut such a fine figure that it soon brought him great distinction in position and wealth . . . a stepping stone to a career of Earldom, serving King Henry VII, Henry VIII, Edward VI and Queen Mary.

QUEEN CHARLOTTE
Hudson

In appreciation for the hospitality shown Joanna and Philip at Wolveton, the Trenchards were sent two Chinese porcelain bowls, probably the first of this kind to come to England.

When we arrived at the castle Mrs. Thimbleby apologized for the absence of her Captain husband, but made us welcome to cover the entire building and roam the grounds at our pleasure. Now we would return to Dorchester.

At Dorchester I would look for some old landmarks . . .especially the grave of Dr. Treves. Recently I read *The Elephant Man*, based on the short life of John Merrick, a nineteenth century deformed human who suffered the disease Multiple Neurofibromatosis. Merrick's trials and tribulations were studied by Dr. Frederick Treves, who discovered that within this grotesque body was a gentle and warm spirit— one that drew admiration from Queen Alexandra (wife of Edward VII) and many princesses. A play was made from the book written by Dr. Treves that lately has won "Best Play of the Year" award on Broadway . . .also in 1980 a successful movie was produced from it.

Dr. Treves, a wonderful humanitarian, was a far-seeing surgeon. Operating for appendicitis was then unheard of. Treves' bold decision to open up his patient and extract the offending member made him famous.

Treves was born at –8 Cornhill Street, Dorchester. When he was seven he started school under the Reverend William Barnes (1801-86). Thomas Hardy, the great novelist, was the companion of Frederick Treves, and both acknowledged the influence that their old master had on their literary works, as Treves was also a prolific writer; some of his titles being: *The Cradle of the Deep, Ugande for a Holiday, The Land That is Desolate, The Ring and the Book (a long narrative poem) and many more. While in Geneva he wrote his last, The Elephant Man and Other Reminiscences* (1923). By now he was very ill with pneumonia. He died there, his body was cremated in Lausanne, and his ashes sent back (after much ordeal in getting the small container through customs—finally having to invoke the authority of the King to get the bit of residue past bureaucratic hodge-podge) to Dorset.

The Society of Dorset Men interred Treves with suitable ceremony in the Dorchester cemetery. The weather

Queen Charlotte's and George III's portraits occupy prominent spaces on the walls of Wolveton.

was vile with driving rain and cold wind. Treves' old friend Thomas Hardy selected the hymns for the burial service. Though Hardy was ill, shaking with a chill, he went nevertheless to the funeral. When he returned home he wrote his last line of poetry (to be published) during his long life. It was entitled "In Memorium Frederici Treves" (Dorchester Cemetery, Jan. 2, 1924).

Treves' finest tribute came from Queen Alexandra (by then the Queen Mother). A cross formed of flowers bore the inscription: For my beloved Sir Frederick Treves, whom we all loved so dearly and now miss so sadly, from his affectionate Alexandra. Sandringham House, Norfolk.

I too would bend over and place a simple wild flower on his humble grave.

We could make it to Clouds Hill, close by, if we hurry. At Wareham, in Dorset, there was the grave of Sir Lawrence of Arabia. His recumbent figure was carved in Purbeck marble on his tomb. His was an enigmatical personality that emerged from a military leadership and a literary background. Clouds Hill was located about ten miles east of Dorchester, near Bovington Camp. This was his 'ivory tower'. All through his Near East campaigns and life on the deserts he secretely coveted a snug corner somewhere by a fireside with his gramaphone and collection of Mozart and Beethoven 78 r.p.m.s. And after the First World War he rented a ramshackled little cottage and fitted it out with his idea of a decor for a man's Utopia.

The campaigns that T.E. Lawrence fought played a leading role that concluded in an armistice that took the Turks out of the war. In 1916 the British had been lowered in prestige by the surrender of the British general, Townshend, in Mesopotamia. But now Lawrence had saved England's face; he knew the Arabs intimately and played on their dislike for their Turkish suzerains. From the conflicts came the independence of the Arabs and a Jewish national state, Israel. In all the troubles of today with these factions, does anyone ever think about the Balfour Declaration in which the British promised the "establishment of a national home for the Jewish people"?

Any way, back to the cottage at Clouds Hill . . It was here that Sir Lawrence wrote his fine book *Seven Pillars of Wisdom*. The living accommodations were sparce and

Lawrence of Arabia was buried in Wareham in Dorsetshire.

everything was on the brownish colour scheme: wooden ceilings and beams and brown leather upholstering. Later, when in 1935 he returned from his discharge in the Air Force Services, he went there to live. He told Lady Astor that wild mares wouldn't drive him from his perfect home, his "earthly paradise". A few days later he was riding from Bovington Camp and had a fatal crash on his motor cycle.

The next day would be taken up in a trip to Cranborne Manor and Breamore House. We'd travel north to Ver-

wood. About three miles northwest of here is Cranborne Manor, the summer home of the Marquis of Salisbury, whose second title is Viscount Cranborne. The site was once a great chase, an immense tract of woodland, but is now a very restricted area. The Viscount is a descendant of Robert Cecil of Hatfield House, First Earl of Salisbury (in Queen Elizabeth I's court). Some important names in the Cecil geneaology are Lady Catherine Howard, Algernon Percy (10th Earl of Northumberland), Lady Mary Catherine Sackville-West, Henry Wellesley (1st. Baron Cowley), James Maitland Balfour, William Cecil (Bishop of Exeter), Elizabeth Vere Cavendish, Edward Cavendish (tenth Duke of Devonshire).

Robert Cecil spent vast amounts of money on building. He started his career of great houses in the reign of Queen Elizabeth I. Among them were Salisbury House (on the banks of the Thames), Theobalds, Burghley House at Stamford, Hatfield and others.

Around the early 1600's Cecil had bought lands in Dorset that included a medieval hunting lodge. He turned this into a small modern country-house. The walls had been gray and unattractively bare, but to them he added tall lattice windows, and sculptured Italian loggias, and for sym-

Cranborne Manor is the summer home of the Marqius of Salisbury, whose second title is Viscount Cranborne. It is built on the land that was once a great chase. The immense tract of woodland is now a very restricted area. The Viscount is a descendant of the illustrious Robert Cecil of Elizabethan fame. Other houses associated with the Cecils are Salisbury House, Theobalds, Burghley House, Hatfield and others.

Cranborne Manor was the hiding place of Angel Clare and Tess of the D'Urbervilles in the Hardy novel.

Burghley House, built by Lord Burghley.

metry he imposed russet brick Jacobean chimneys. It became a fine house that expressed all the romantic strains of an Elizabethan imagination that could produce *A Midsummer Night's Dream.*

The present owner of Cranborne Manor is Lord David Cecil, C.H. Hon.D.Litt. He is a former professor of English Literature at Oxford, President of the Poetry Society and Rede Lecturer at Cambridge University. He is author of many books on historical and literary subjects.

The afternoon that we visited the manor a fete was being held for charity, and Lord Cecil made an appearance among the guests. The object of our visit was for a different reason, though. Thomas Hardy had made Cranborne Manor the setting of an episode in *Tess of the D'Urbervilles.* In their attempt to escape justice after Tess murdered Alex, Tess and Angel Clare fled from Sandbourne (Bournemouth) through New Forest then northeastward until they came to a large house that was vacant. They crawled through a window and remained there in sumptuous comfort until suspicions were aroused in a villager who went at certain times to open and close the windows of the house. This was Cranborne Manor.

From here we headed west to Breamore House. Breamore village lies on the high road from Fordingbridge to Salisbury. In A.D. 519 a great battle was fought here. A half a mile away is Breamore Down where the leaders of the Saxon invaders under Cerdic slaughtered 5000 Britons and their king, Natan-leod, who, according to legends of Wessex, is buried here. Close by stands the church of Breamore, surrounded by a beautiful setting of old picturesque trees. From 980 to 1130 there isn't much information about the building, but from the mid-twelfth century there is a complete history kept by the Augustine Priory who took it over then. In 1536 Thomas Cromwell, the king's agent in abolishing the Monasteries, gave a good report on this particular Austin Canon, "that they are of good conversion", and spared it. But smaller houses were suppressed in the area. In 1538 properties including the rectories and chapels plus the manor of Breamore were granted to Henry, Marquis of Exeter. At that time a Priory was connected, but now only the bare site can still be seen adjoining the River Avon and Breamore Hill. Excavations there revealed traces of the cloisters and some stone coffins, three of which are standing beside the

172

old yew tree in Breamore churchyard. I wasn't a bit squeamish eating my cheese sandwich and leaning back on the grave boxes . . . they must have been at least six hundred years old.

The present structure of the manor is an important example of a Saxon building dating from the late tenth century, and added to until 1922, when the four bells were recast

using most of the original metal. The house was open this time when we visited it, last year we picked the wrong day for viewing. Breamore House was built in 1583. For over 200 years it was the home of Sir Edward Hulse and heirs. Hulse was George II's physician.

It is built of faded red brick laid in a two-dimensional square pattern, called *diapered*, in two different colours — and a roof full of gables and tall chimneys. The natural wooded park gives it a charming appearance. I was excitied, recently, when I recognized it in a T.V. production of *Barchester Towers* by Trollope.

The interior was impressive; the rooms were large and panelled in dark carved woodwork. The house had been faithfully restored in 1856 after being ravaged by fire. There was a marvelous display of fine furniture including

Elizabethan carved oak tables with bulbous, intricately decorated legs; Jacobean chairs with embroidered tapestry bottoms; marble consoles holding beautiful vases and coffeepots by Wedgewood; Ming china bowls; interesting pieces of inlaid boxes; clocks of all periods and Chelsea procelain figurines. The most outstanding attraction was the picture collection. The upstair dining walls were covered in paintings, and the one commanding my attention was a full size portrait of a young man—the son of Guy Fawkes, the leader of a most infamous rebellion, a celebrated plot in English history. In past times many communities observed Guy Fawkes Day on November 5th by lighting bonfires and tossing a straw effigy of old Fawkes into the flames. In fact, Daphne du Maurier's most recent novel opens with "Mad's" foster children making a figure of the villian to burn in their fire. This was *Rule Britannia.*

It was like this: in 1603 James I created for Robert Cecil (beloved right hand of Queen Elizabeth) the title of Lord Cecil, and two years later Earl of Salisbury. He had a knack of sniffing out brewing conspiracies. Elizabeth had left the religious question somewhat settled, but with King James (his mother being a staunch Catholic)—the Catholic factions began to take heart in a restoration of Popery, or at least a relaxing of the laws against them. Early in his reign he managed to alienate feelings between the parties of Scottish Presbyterians . . . having had his fill of Presbyterian extremism as a boy in Scotland. There were certain Englishmen who hated the Anglican settlement and wanted the country to go one way or the other: Presbyterian or Catholic. Burghley (Robert Cecil) was the watchdog, trying to keep peace, but he believed the single Anglican Church should be broad enough to tolerate many shades of opinion.

There was a powerful group of men—they had already engaged in the Bye and Main Plots — who were now ready to do something more serious. Cecil had been getting whiffs of their activities, but bided his time. And then a youthful peer of Parliament, Lord Monteagle took the note to Lord Salisbury (Cecil), who took it to James I. The letter was understood to imply that there was a planned conspiracy to blow up Parliament. People were sent to search Parliament's basement and there was Guy Fawkes with barrels of gunpowder. All involved in the plot were rounded up, tried and

Portrait of Guy Fawkes' son hangs at Breamore House.

174

executed. The only admirable thing about the whole mess was the way the accused stood up silently under the dire torture they suffered—hanged, drawn, and quartered. After this episode, measures were taken to weaken the Roman Catholics. This cured them of any future ideas about starting a rebellion.

Incidentally, the son of Guy Fawkes was the first cricket player in England, so that must have entitled him to a prominent place over the mantle of the Drawing Room. It had been a pleasureable day, and we'd be back at the Caledonian Hotel in Bournemouth for dinner on time. Afterwards we walked to the edge of the English Channel and watched the sun setting behind the interesting silhouette of the city. On returning we were brought our hot chocolate before retiring.

The next morning would be spent in the New Forest. The wild ponies seemed to have doubled in population in the past year . . . Dick stopped the car and pushed the posterior of the stupid beast off the road, honking the horn had been useless. There is enough to occupy you for the entire day here—sightseeing at Burley (a village in the Forest) with browsing in the craftshops, antique-hunting and taking pictures. Lunch was at Rhinefield House (once owned by Queen Victoria), then we walked the nature trails until supper time, which we took at The Queen's Head Restaurant back in Burley.

Each day found us returning to some lovely place where we had visited so many times. The following one was too beautiful to be spent anywhere but on the beach of the English Channel. We had to walk two blocks through the delightful Boscombe Park to get to the water's edge. Roses were in full bloom in all colours, including lavender—which I thought too funereal to be pretty. Finding a vacant space on the sand, we plopped down to watch the scenery go by. There were several Chinese vessels, called junks, with very high poop, overhanging stern and delicate pole masts bearing orange and turquoise sails gliding on the water. As the sun rose higher and the heat began to beat down, I reminisced on what all we had left behind on the cool Devon moors, and I thought of Charlotte Bronte when she wrote, describing her sister Emily's love of the moors, "flowers brighter than the rose bloomed in the blackest of the heath for her—

out of a sullen hollow in a livid hillside, her mind could make an Eden.'' I could see the tall hedgerows and wet green fields contrasting with the bleak wildness of the Dartmoor and wished I were back on the farm at Sticklepath. Do you remember the lines from *Wuthering Heights* that go, ''the north wind blowing over the edge—a few stunted firs—a range of gaunt thorns all stretching their limbs one way, as if craving alms of the sun'' (They apply to the Dartmoors also.) Oh, the moors at Gidleigh! . . . and I want to return now. Bournemouth is nice for some people, but the Riviera aspect of it is not *My England.*

The time flew by in Bournemouth and now we leave for Gatwick, south of London. There would be much to do in that area. Highway 31 would route us through Ringwood, Romsey, Winchester, Alton, Guildford . . . and then on the A 25 we'd reach Dorking (an adorable old town, but we'd not stop, as the next day we had planned to return from Gatwick and visit our friends who owned Pixie House). We made a short cut by dropping south and winding our way to Horley, close to Gatwick Terminal.

Burley, a village in the New Forest, is populated with wild horses. This indigneous breed, protected by the Crown since William I's time, is one of the attractions to this area.

177

Patrick, our doorman friend of many past summers, helped us with our luggage and got us settled. After a nap we drove to Newdigate, the village where Patrick lived, close to Charlwood. We learned from him of the beautiful old church of St. Peters that was built in 1180 on part of the de Warrenne's ancient estate. It has been kept in good repair over the eight hundred years and added on to, keeping the original form. Many gravestones covered the nave floor, one (William de Newdigate's, 1377) bears the arms of its occupant, three lion's paws. The parish chest, made of a single piece of oak and closed with the traditional three locks, contains the stored parish records going back eight hundred years. The carved angels on the choir stalls and the poppy heads on the front pews were done by pupils of Mrs. Janson, who set up a woodworking class at her home, Newdigate Place, in 1902. She also did the needlework by the south door.

We called the Sullivans and would see them the next day at Dorking. I guess it's sentimental . . . but I am only creating pictures in my mind when I travel: images that later

I can muse on and delight over in some nostalgic reverie of the past. I will never forget the day spent with our two English friends, Kay and Terry. Both had lived their early adult days in war-torn country . . . she a nurse and he in the battle lines. There was much to learn first-hand about the war during the nineteen-forties. Terry wanted us to see the most beautiful spot in Surrey, so he drove us up to Leith Hill, that started almost in his backyard. It was tea time so he spread a blanket, then took out the big basket containing two thermos bottles of hot tea, home-baked sultana raisin bread, and sweet butter. No gourmet kitchen could produce more satisfying morsels, nor could there be found such a bewitching setting anywhere in the world. The scene takes one back to 851 when the Danes had sacked Canterbury and London, then when moving on to Winchester they encountered King Ethelwulf (Alfred the Great's father). Ethelwulf secured the advantage by occupying the greater heights of Leith Hill and was thereby victorious. Of more recent time I like to think of George Meredith, on the close-by range to the north, doing his best writing at Juniper Hall on Box Hill, and during the French Revolution Madame de Staël and Tallerand seeking refuge here. So, somewhere in our minds we'll store up the memory of heavenly hills and glades for a future taking out and day-dreaming over —some winter day when the bashful sun has hid behind his cloud curtain . . . and I'm just plain home-sick for England.

After tea we drove through the scenic village of Shere. On the great heights of Leith Hill there is a tower (64 ft.) from which, on a good day, one can see the Kentish hills and even the English Channel. The tower was built in 1766 by Richard Hill, and at one time was furnished, but now is in delapidated state. We didn't go into the seventeenth century mansion close by, but were told it contained a rare collection of early Wedgewood china and portraits by Romney, Stubbs, and Reynolds. It is open to the public at certain times. In this area the North Downs reach their highest peak and are dotted with silver birches, golden gorse and yellow broom; and nestled down in this fairy woodland is the pretty village of Shere with the river Tillingsborne flowing through. There is a stock pillar at the old inn in the center of town where nagging wives of the medieval days were punished when they caused offense (while the poor 'innocent and abused husband' sat in the nearby pub and quaffed his ale midst his commiserating cronies!) Now trailing geraniums swing in baskets from its frame while female publicans (pub owners) scowl at their male customers all they please.

We parted with the Sullivans and left for our hotel at Gatwick. Tomorrow we would visit Knole House at Seven Oaks in Kent county.

To reach Knole take the M23 (as much as I dislike the busy motorways) and go north until you reach the local #25, then turn east to Godstone. If you are interested in the eighteenth century political writers you will want to go two miles north of here to find a quaint old inn associated with William Cobbett. Someone spoke of *Peter Porcupine*—and I would have said that it was the title of one of his witty and sarcastic writings, such as Jonathon Swift wrote . . . maybe like a *Tale of a Tub* or *Gullivar's Travels*. I blushed when informed that P. Porcupine was Cobbett's pseudonym. Cobbett was born at Farnham, some forty miles to the west, and at an early age joined the British Army. He later deserted to write articles exposing the abuse and cruelty in the army. He had difficulty proving his allegations when suit was brought against him, so he fled to the U.S.A. where he remained for eight years publishing journals to promote reform in the military system. The rest of his life he see-sawed back and forth from England to America still urging for Parliamentary reforms. Some of his works are *Rural Rides* (1830), and *A Year's Residence In the United States of America* (1818).

Continue on to Westerham, a small town pleasantly situated near the source of the Darent River. General Wolfe was born here in 1727 in the vicarage, which is now known as Quebec House, where the descendants of the family still reside. Visitors are freely admitted. In the village square is a statue of the hero—and close by, a vendor had set up his stand selling the best piping hot fish and chips I have ever tasted . . . I drool at the remembrance of them. The location of Westerham has literary associations with Jane Austen, as the parsonage of Mr. Collins in *Pride and Prejudice* was in Hundsford, not far away.

Now, remaining on road 25 we head toward Seven Oaks. Upon arriving at the railroad station turn southeast. Knole is one and half miles farther. Well, here in the lovely wooded park is the largest and finest baronial mansion in England, and except for the church snatchings of Henry VIII and his man Cranmer, it would still belong to the archbishops of Canterbury, whose Abp. built it in 1454. When Elizabeth I came to the throne she turned it over to her cousin Thomas Sackville, first Earl of Dorset. In its present form the house dates mainly from the time of James I—and its interior fittings and decor are practically unchanged. The main rooms shown are the Great Hall with portraits by Van Dyck and the ancient statue of the Greek Demosthenes; the Brown Gallery hung with Holbeins; the Billiard Room with its curious old table; the Leicester Gallery; Lady Betty Germain's Rooms; the Spangled Bedroom; the King's Bedroom (as fixed up by James I); the Venetion Bedchamber; the Crimson Drawing Room; Ball Room; and the Dining Room . . which by now had worn me out. I was sated with art works by everybody! I didn't visit the Cartoon Room (Raphael's) or the Chapel. I'd met my match in staggering show-pieces—such a crush of too much.

The family of Sackville-West married into many established names, mainly the Cecils of Hatfield, whose descendants are among the Baron Harlechs, the Cavendishes and the present David Cecil, C.H. (son of Lady Cecily Alice Gore, 4th Marchioness of Salisbury), well known author. Tomorrow we will visit Sissinghurst Castle where V. Sackville-West and her husband Harold Nicolson have transformed a wasteland into an Eden. But now, since Ightham Mote (Igam) is so close, let's have a look.

The village of Ightham is delightful; there are Tudor houses and shops on the main street and a tea-room dating from the twelve hundreds. The old church of St. Peter's, of the fourteenth century, stands on a little hill nearby. One of the few moated houses remaining in England is two miles from the center of the village. It is called Ightham Mote (deriving from 'moot') because it was a council place where moot questions were settled in medieval times. Most of its original appearance has survived, though the interior has been altered to accommodate modern demands for comfort. It is a lived-in house, but is open at certain times for visitors. The courtyard, Great Hall, Solar Room and crypt may be seen just as they were first built.

We've taken in enough for one day, so back to the

hotel. That evening we dined at an old inn built in Henry V's day. Accessible by foot—it could be seen from our bedroom window—we shot across the hazardous motorway and, by cutting through a field, came upon an unexpected ancient graveyard attached to a jewel of an old church. As the restaurant didn't open till eight o'clock we killed a half hour prowling about the sanctuary that was lit up by the western sun back of the stained windows. By then we were well in the mood to appreciate almost anything served up. The Bull's Inn was quaint in the extreme. To enter the area of the buffet one had to almost double-up to duck under the low roof beam. But the culinary offering was worthy of a little exertion. There was a choice of sitting inside or outdoors. We took the latter and shared a table with English people, which added to the evening's pleasure. The British sense of humor is refreshing to me . . . rather naive, but charming. In our group one fellow who seemed something of a buffoon piped out to another chap at the end of the table, "Aye say, did you here this one? Mama and Papa Tomato went for a walk, baby Tomato kept lagging behind. Mama Tomato hurried back to reprimand son: 'to-day you hang behind—tomorrow you be tomato catsup' ". And you wouldn't believe that this spinner of inaneness was a moment before quoting Heine and Hegel. (Maybe the vegetarian comedy was for the benefit of the two Americans present).

The next day was to be a high spot on our list of sights to see; we would go to Sissinghurst Castle. The story of Sissinghurst is a short one: once there was a lovely Tudor mansion that nobody took care of and it fell to pieces. In the seventeen hundreds it became a prison for French soldiers. The French referred to it as *le chateau* and the name stuck.

The site was lived on as early as the twelfth century. At that time it was Saxingherete. Where the orchard now grows was the manor—and of such large size that Edward I and his retinue spent four nights here in 1305. Later the Bakers of Cranbrook bought it and tore it down, building another one slightly to its west. The owner was a colorful figure called "Bloody Baker" because of alleged cruelty to Protestants, rape, murder, and pillage. When he died he left a huge fortune to his son, Sir Richard Baker, who constructed the tower which stands today as the main feature of the

The towers at Sissinghurst Gardens, developed by the Sackville-Wests in 1930.

182

garden. When the Civil War came, a later son backed the wrong side and lost everything. Horace Walpole visited the place in 1752 and found the "park in ruins and a house in ten times worse shape." It was at this time that the Government leased the property and turned it into a prison. To be sent to Sissinghurst was considered the harshest fate that could be endured by the French seamen at the hands of the English during the Seven Years' War.

Between its infamous years and the early twentieth century it existed as a work house for farm laborers. In 1930 V. Sackville-West, well-known novelist, poet, biographer and gardener, a descendant of the original Bakers, was searching for a place to make a new garden. Her own home, Long Barn, near Seven Oaks was threatened by a new road development that would be unsightly. When she saw Sissinghurst and the rich soil she selected this spot. The results are a beautiful haven of flowers, arbors, and walkways that terminate in marble statues. There are the spring garden (March to May), early summer garden (May to July), later summer garden (July to August) and an autumn garden (September-October). Whichever one you catch will be a sensational experience.

It's a jolt to leave the twentieth century and plunge back into the thirteen hundreds by going to Bodiam Castle, but here we go. The A229 goes to Hawkhurst; find A265 and by heading southwest you will come to Bodiam. Bodiam is everyone's dream of how a castle should look. It is England's brightest jewel. The country is a bit more hilly around here . . . the Rother river flows at the castle's edge and that is why the fortifications were built; the French could easily approach their enemy by crossing the Channel to Rye, on the coast of England, then sailing up the Rother. King Richard II gave license for Bodiam to be constructed in 1385. It wasn't brought into use at this time, but did see military action twice later—the last time was during the Civil War when the Parliamentary Army under General Waller besieged it and "slighted" it, leaving the castle merely a shell. But what a beauty, the outside in perfect condition. On nearing it one sees a lovely water-lily lake with a massive castle seeming to float on its surface . . . completely extraordinary!

A museum on the grounds displays all the artifacts found during excavation within its walls.

Now to Penshurst. There are some qualities about

184

Southeast England that make it different from the rest of the Island because ages ago this area extended from Dover into Hampshire, over a hundred and forty-five miles. It was called the Forest of Anderida—one vast forest—which is now known as the Weald. The three main counties are Surrey, Sussex, and Kent . . . but acutally there is more land than the shires mentioned here. New Forest in Hampshire gives a good idea of what it once was like. From findings of the archaeologist, shards of pottery and such, we know that it took about two dozen guides to lead the Kings of the thirteenth and fourteenth century on their Royal Progresses through the forest from London eastward to Dungeness.

But civilization grew faster in the southeast than in other sections, and men of energy soon moved toward land exploitation and needed castles with protective moats about them. They can still be seen in this area. Saxons, Jutes, Celts, Romans and Normans all contributed in taming the wilderness. Needing timber and iron for their structures and later for ships, they began to denude the land, so its great forests

Penshurst.

disappeared. By the time Elizabeth I came to the throne it was necessary to make laws rationing the cutting of oaks. There isn't much iron left today, but what is in the sub-soil contributes to the richness of the ground, producing fruits, cereals, and hops in abundance. Hence, Kent is called the "Garden of England".

In the midst of this garden we find Penshurst. One might spend the entire day here, walking the lanes and paths of the surrounding countryside. The village has kept much of its Tudor appearance, many of the buildings are from three to four hundred years old. The church of St. John the Baptist was built in the eleven hundreds, and its bent and weathered timbers can still be seen. The family of the great poet Sir Phillip Sidney added the last chapel in 1820 — the third one to be constructed.

Penshurst Place has been the ancestral home of the Sidneys since the mid-sixteenth century. Two hundred years later the male line of the Sidneys, who had become the Earls of Leicester, died out and the female line of Shelleys claimed the property and took the Sidney name. Percy B. Shelley was a kinsman of this branch.

The most impressive room is the Baron's Great Hall. It is fourteenth century and the proportions and vast height of the chestnut roof are marvelous. Wooden figures around the walls are supposed to be the retainers of its medieval owners. The green velvet bedroom of the 'Blessed Sir Phillip Sidney' is shown, and on a table near the fireplace is a death-mask of Queen Elizabeth I. In this casting her real appearance is portrayed and looks very much like the artist's interpretations.

The grounds of Penshurst are charming and worth an hour's strolling. But we missed Lamberhurst, between Bodiam and Penshurst . . .we'll get back there on our visit to Eastbourne. Lingfield is on the way to Gatwick and I'd like to see where the Cobham family had lived in the fourteen hundreds. The first time I was in Lingfield, a dozen years earlier, the quaint parish church was just another church . . . one of hundreds we'd seen . . . and the three tombs like all the rest.

After a visit to Lincoln Cathedral and seeing the beautiful statue of Alfred L. Tennyson by Watts something happened. On the plinth was a short poem:

Flower in the crannied wall
I pluck you out of the crannies,
I hold you here, root and all, in my hand,
Little flower—but if I could understand
What you are, root and all, and all in all
I should know what God and man is.

John Oldcastle, Lord Cobham

On returning home I took out my complete works of Tennyson and the volume fell open at *Sir John Oldcastle, Lord Cobham.* I began reading and couldn't put the book down. I read the poem over three more times and it started having some meaning for me. I dare say that it is void of sense, pointless, if one knows nothing of the background of the Protestant Movement . . .in all its agonies . . . or the lineage of English kings, but I started researching on the subjects, and through this study my life has become much richer. One needs to know the setting to appreciate this poetical work.

In the reign of Edward IV, England had never known such corrupt days. The King himself set the example by his 'filthie sin of lechery and fornication, with abominable adultries.' Richard III followed in his steps . . . and England had become the most lawless country in existence. They had just concluded the Hundred Years' War with France, and the returning soldiers continued their fighting ways among the nobility of their homeland. Greed and lust abounded everywhere. Even judges were 'bought off' and juries were paid to be friendly to the highest bidder . . . be he plantiff or defendant.

Chaucer also was influcened—he pretended one thing and practiced another. And his attire was as whacky as the next fellow's: one blue stocking and one green attached to \balloon-like pants of embroidered material topped with fancy jackets and slashed sleeves.

Taxes were on everything, including necessities like salt. Torture of both witness *and* accused was developed by Edward IV and continued through the next two hundred years. People thought of nothing but their amusement.

Women were loose, the cities were dens of thieves, the poor were miserable and all were subject to the Pope . . . even to the practice of kissing his feet. It was truly a time of the Lord of Misrule—and surely a time for a man like Wiclif! To be very brief one could really say that politics of the day paved the way for the eventual Reformation. Wiclif was at Oxford University. The year was 1360; he was master of Balliol College, ordained to the priesthood. He was alarmingly prolific in his literary outpourings on theology, attracting the attention of John of Gaunt (King Richard II's uncle). Gaunt belonged to an anticlerical party at the court, and resented the great amounts of money going to the Pope—and the fact that large sums found their way to cardinals in France who enjoyed good food and bad women . . . while England was engaged in war with so little in the treasury to arm and feed the soldiers. Gaunt allied himself with Wiclif . . . which saved Wiclif from dying a martyr's death later. The tracts of the reformer became so dangerous as to encourage revolution. He wrote, "any person in a state of grace shares with God the ownership of all goods—that everything should be held by the righteous in common."

This was interpreted as a 'theoretical communism and anarchism.' Bishop Courteney, leader of the clerical group, attacked Wiclif after a series of sermons in London, and summoned him to appear before a council of prelates in 1377. Wiclif was condemned on eighteen counts (from his treatise *On Civil Dominion*) and ordered by the Pope to be arrested and kept in chains.

When Parliament met, a majority of its members being anticlerics, they reckoned that if the King could keep the wealth that was being sent out of the country it would solve their armaments problem in their troubles with France. So Wiclif ended his days quietly at the rectory at Lutterworth. Now I knew what the lines in Tennyson's poem *Sir John Oldcastle, Lord Cobham* meant:

> Not least art thou, little Bethlehem
> In Judah, for in thee the Lord was born;
> Nor thou in Britain, Little Lutterworth,
> Least, for in thee the word was born again.

191

Wiclif's greatest achievement was in translating the Scriptures and paving the way for Luther, Calvin and others.

Oh, there's lots more to it than that—and it makes interesting reading—but I'm a traveller, not a scholar. Getting back to Tennyson and Lord Cobham, whose family built the church at Lingfield: by 1407 the Church began to grow stronger, having matured a bit from Wiclif's teaching. When Henry V came to the throne in 1413, one of his closest friends was Lord Cobham (Sir John Oldcastle). Lord Cobham served his country well in his position, but he also protected the Lollard preachers (followers of Wiclif) of whom there were many in Kent and Herefordshire. He ignored several summons from the bishops, but responded to a writ from the King—and stood examination in the very chapter house where Wiclif had been tried thirty-odd years before. He would not reject the Lollards in their views on the Eucharist or Confessional—so he was condemned and sent to the Tower of London. Some Lollards, upon hearing this, became militaristic and tried to seize the King, but were defeated, and of course hanged. Lord Cobham escaped and hid for three years in Wales. In the end he was captured and burned as a traitor and heretic on Christmas Day 1417.

Tennyson's poem is the story of this Lord Cobham— and it took all this research and three tombs in the little parish church at Lingfield for me to understand its contents. If I could write an epitaph for this great man it would be:

When the word of the Lord became flesh
Then it was martyrs fell afresh.

The sun was getting low as we returned to Gatwick. I haven't mentioned this before but Gatwick had its first publicity as an important R.A.F. station during the last war. It grew to include a race-course nearby, and after the war it was turned into commercial use. It is located halfway between Brighton and London. In 1958 it opened as an international airport—the most modern in Europe; it combined rail, road, and air facilities under one roof. It has continued to grow and now one hundred companies operate from here, and have as many as three hundred aircraft movements every day during peak seasons.

192

When landing, after a long night over the Atlantic Ocean, it is a comfort to know that after collecting luggage at the carousel there will be a courtesy limousine driving up every thirty minutes to take you to your hotel . . . be it any of the half dozen fine ones close by. After all, it's about two o'clock in the morning in the U.S.A. and time to retire — while England has just started its busy eight a.m. traffic nightmares. If you are over forty I'd say don't begin your exploring at this hour . . . and on the wrong side of the road too! Go to bed for a while . . . after awakening have lunch at one of the quaint inns close by, do a little joy riding to get used to the feel of the car . . . then call it a day. If you pick up some sweet rolls you can enjoy a light snack in the hotel room as all the fixings for tea or coffee are there for the plugging in. Television reception is superb in this area and program choice is endless. Next morning you will be in shape to conquer the Island!

And we arose to a beautiful morning. Starting south we came to Haywards Heath, in the midst of the agriculture centre. A Civil War battle was fought on Minster Green; the Royalist were scattered with a loss of over two hundred men. There are some beautiful gardens in the vicinity. Borde Hill, about two miles to the north, is filled with rare plants, camellias, magnolias, and herbs. To the southwest is Heaslands with its delightful water gardens, walled gardens, waterfowls and roses everywhere. To the east is Sheffield Park with its many lakes. Haywards Heath is a nice place to stop to eat, and also shop for needlework. Going southward toward Lewes we find Glyndebourne, a spot of muscial renown. In 1934 John Christie, who had taught science at Eton, and was a lover of fine music, added onto his ancestral home an auditorium to present first-class opera sung by world-famous singers. The season is from May to August, and formal dress is required. Supper may be brought in picnic basket from home or bought in the dining room. The restaurant was carefully designed to protect the oak trees that grow through the roof.

Our schedule did not allow for an evening's stop for the opera, and neither did our wardrobe include the proper attire. I remember once, however, that at the Savoy in London it was quite simple to adapt a plain dark jumper by adding a lovely flower, string of pearls (imitations) and high

heels . . . Dick got by with a dark suit (no sports jackets—
please) and a good tie.

We were in a hurry to get to Seaford on the coast east
of us. Intentions were to see Mr. Desmond Kyne. We had
met him nine years before at a 'bed and breakfast'. Our
hostess had to leave for the night and left her house with
the three of us. A neighbor came over the next morning to
fix our eggs and bacon. Mr. Kyne provided us with the most
interesting evening explaining a special engraving process
which he had perfected. He had many samples of his art work
with him, as this was a business trip he was on. His discoveries
in the usage of kinetic engraving were put to stunning results.
At this time he was using as subjects the knights and ladies
of medieval history. "I have carried out a study by microscopy
of patterns in nature which are not immediately apparent
to the human eye, concentrating my work especially upon
periodic gridline structures", he said, and trying to clear up
this technical jargon added, "let me give you some examples
of wonderful things that nature has done with this principle.
Occasionally, while digging in the garden or turning a stone,
a small black beetle will be disturbed and as he scuttles away
one notices how his black shell is sometimes green, sometimes
blue. There are fish whose scales produce similar effects;
butterflies and some moths have much the same kind of pattern embodied in their wing structures . . . the principle
behind these various effects is commonly found in nature.
The techniques employed are the most advanced of their kind
in the world, dealing with light refraction and reflection.
What is accomplished is an iridescence on a metal material
(aluminum, generally) of a luminescence such as you see when
looking through a stained glass window. However there is
no light behind this surface—it merely gives the appearance
of illumination."

I was fascinated with the beautiful work. Our friend
lived in Seaford, about nine miles east of Brighton and this
would take us on a coastal route that was new to us; I had
long wanted to visit the white cliffs called 'Seven Sisters'
at Seaford. Not too far to the east were our old haunts
. . . Eastbourne, Pevensey, Bexhill, St. Leonards and
Hastings . . . all on the English Channel. From Hastings,
following the coast, you will see Rye Bay (some three miles
north is the quaint old port of Rye), then passing Hythe and

*Our Lady of Knock is an
example of kinetic engraving, resembling a stained
glass window.*

194

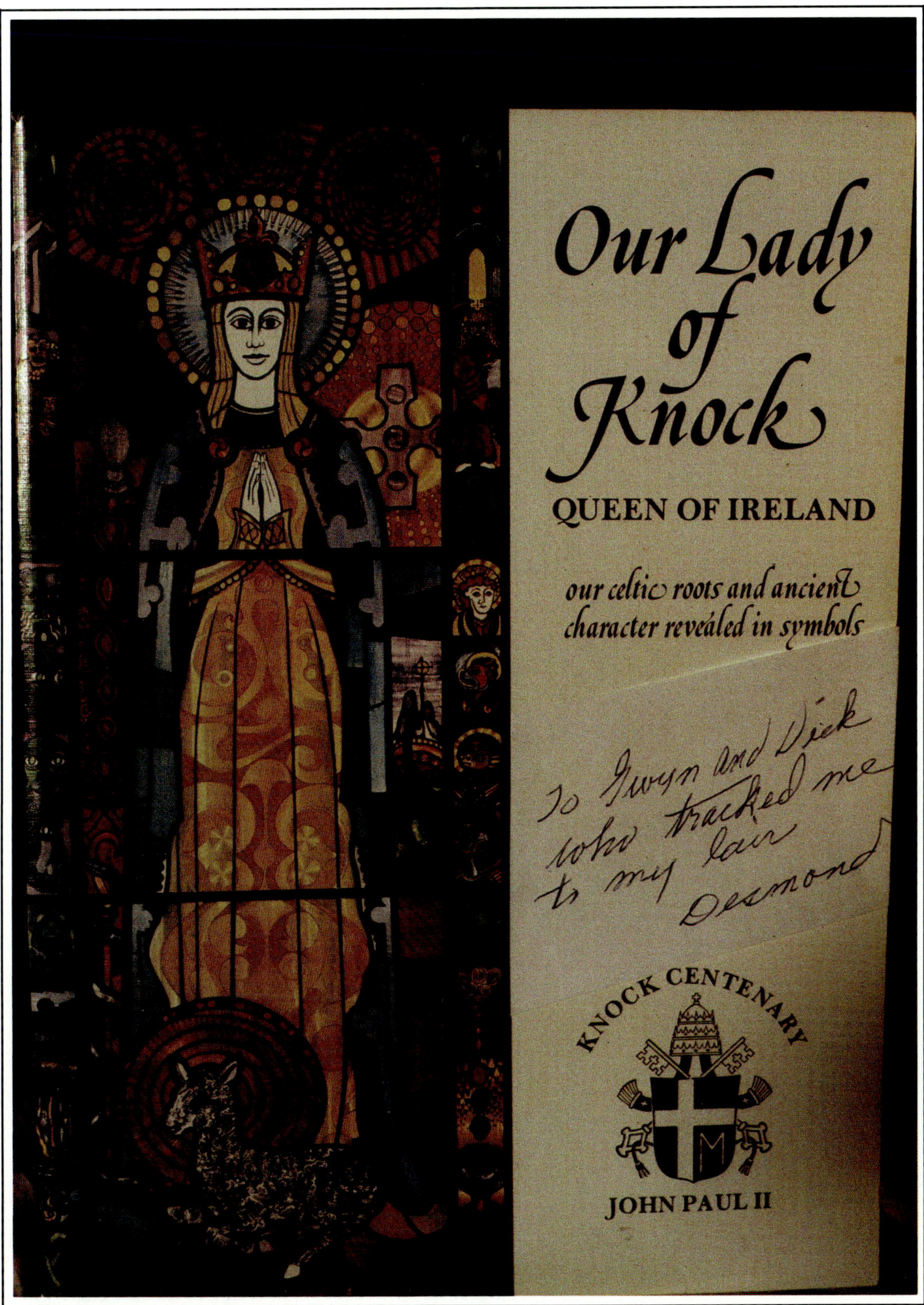
Our Lady
of
Knock
QUEEN OF IRELAND
our celtic roots and ancient
character revealed in symbols
To Gwyn and Dick
who tracked me
to my lair
Desmond
KNOCK CENTENARY
JOHN PAUL II

Folkestone you will reach Dover. At Dover the Channel may be crossed to Zeebrugge and Ostende, in Belguim or Dunkerque, Calais and Boulogne in France. In 1973 we boarded a hovercraft at Dover for Calais . . . it was a quiet crossing, but the next summer the same craft sank in the Channel. So the waters there can get rambunctious at times! But back to Seaford.

We had rather surprised Mr. Kyne with our visit—but he beamed radiantly upon seeing us, and already had the teapot brewing. Mrs. Kyne brought out the biscuits . . . and a lovely visit we had.

"Ever since completing art school in London", our host said, "I have resisted an urge to make a picture of the Virgin Mary . . . and I have kept putting it off until one day, while I was in Ireland, I was driving from Galway to Sligo on a dark winter's evening; the inspiration hit me to do it *now!* Thirty years had passed since I had been a small boy pushing my way on a bicycle along this same road. As memories flooded back, they were sharply altered by the sight of a great Basilica, cradled impressively amidst low surrounding hills. This was Knock, but very different from what I remembered of it. I knew with certitude that a response was

The ferry leaves Dover for a docking in Oostende.

196

asked for, and that the time had come for me to make my composition.

"Some days later, while visiting Maynooth University I met Fr. Ledwith, one of the professors who was deeply interested in ancient Celtic civilization. I soon found myself resolved to start my project . . . an Icon of the Virgin. Having seen so many weak images that dishonoured Mary, I cringed at the thought of my failure to portray her greatness. But when I had completed the work—the size of a house door—it was accepted, and now hangs in the Basilica of Our Lady Queen of Ireland."

Others have been made since then . . . one for Queen Elizabeth II, the Pope, and the President of the U.S.A.

After tea he walked with us to the cliffs, but by now the sun was not good for photography. The earth here, as along so much of the coastline, is of chalky composition with the land undulating into hills and depressions made by ancient rivers that drained into the Channel. The pounding waves and weather have combined to form a dramatic sight. . .more impressive than the White Cliffs of Dover. Inland, about four miles north, is the Wilmington Man—or Long Man—cut into the turf by the Saxons. It is being preserved by concrete blocks laid in 1969. We would have to take the car to see it as there are so many interesting things between here and there. Parting with the Kynes, we decided to meet them the next day at Eastbourne for lunch.

This line of beach holds little for the sailor . . . he will generally skip Bexhill, Eastborne and Pevensey Bay and make for Beachy Head, a very notorious and uncanny spot where many persons throw themselves from the extremely high cliffs each year.

The next day, as arranged, our friends were awaiting us in front of the restaurant at Eastborne. Sheltered by the South Downs and Beachy Head is Eastbourne, a very prosperous and popular seaside resort. The beach stretches three miles along the shore. A mile or so inland is the old village where you find Devonshire Park, famous for tennis tournaments. Between the old and new town lies Compton Place, built in the seventeen hundreds by the Dukes of Devonshire, to whom Eastbourne owes its development and progress. There are several well-known schools here and many other attractions including numerous walks along the cliffs. Adjoining it is Lullington with probably the smallest church in England (sixteen squre feet). From here we drove back to see the Wilmington Man, cut out of the white chalk. He is a two hundred and forty ft. figure and carries a staff in each hand. Many think he was carved by the Celts and represents Baldur, a symbol of spring.

We left our friends here and set out for Pevensey where we would spend a night before continuing our journey eastward to Hastings. After selecting a B. and B. we settled the over-night bag and started to explore, stopping first at Pevensey Castle. It stands in an enclosure of ten acres surrounded by a Roman wall. Round towers, some twenty feet high, have been there for eleven hundred years. This site was identified with the Roman Anderida, a great fort that was taken in 401 by the Saxons. Pevensey Bay, nearby, is the accepted landing-place of William the Conqueror in 1066. The old Mint House is nearly six hundred years old. . . now a shop. We would still have time to drive four miles north to Hurstmonceux Castle. (Many years ago we took a pleasure boat from Charing Cross Pier to Greenwich, passing wonderful sights along the way, and docked close to where the famous clipper *Cutty Sark* was anchored. We went to the Royal Naval College and the National Maritime Museum that included Queen Anne's House, designed by Inigo Jones for the consort of James I, Anne of Denmark. The Greenwich Park rises at the rear of these buildings from which location one can see all of East London. At the highest point of the hill is the former Royal Observatory which used to establish the Greenwich Standard Time, but in 1950 the work of the observatory was transferred to Hurstmonceux.)

It was too late for visitors to see inside (or maybe never are admitted). The exterior was beautiful—and if anything could surpass Bodiam Castle in picturesqueness it might be Hurstmonceux. It was built about 1440 and stands surrounded by an expansive moat. Originally it was to have been a fortified manor house but in the eighteenth century it was dismantled and later redone in the 1930's. We had enough time to wander over to the parish church—a quarter of a mile away—where there are canopied tombs of the Dacre family . . . some dating back to the early fourteen hundreds. A hundred years later their names crop up with the Percys

and the Nevilles over Catholic matters during the Dissolution.

We wanted to be bright and bushy-tailed for tomorrow's adventures. The next morning over coffee, sausage, bacon, eggs, mushrooms and marmalade I looked out on the coast of Pevensey and could imagine the Duke of Normandy and his fine army springing ashore from their boats wearing splendid armour—and all the barons with painted shields and pointed helmets. Meeting them in the fields near Hastings would be the wild savage-looking Saxons with golden hair blowing in the wind, carrying round hide-shields, and their legs wound with leather thongs. The wretched day would end at sunset with Harold of the Saxons falling with an arrow through his eye. This was over nine hundred years ago.

Three miles north west of Hastings, on the local 2204, is the scene of the Battle of Hastings on Senlac Hill. To look on the quiet hills and fields you would never know it to be the bloody site of the siege that sealed the fate of England. She was to become Norman now instead of Saxon. The abbey

200

with its massive gateway that stands at the entrance of High
Street dominates the town.

In 1066 William of Normandy vowed that he would
erect a church here if God would give him the victory. The
high altar would be the spot where Harold II fell in battle.
William kept his word. But much later, after Henry VIII's
Dissolution of the abbeys the property was given to Sir
Anthony Browne who immediately pulled it down. Only the
crypt of William's church still exists, also the roofless
refectory built by the Benedictines . . . which is interesting
to visit. Excavations were conducted and the location of the
high altar was found and rebuilt in 1903 by the Souvenir
Normandy members. The story of that battle is so well known
that I hesitate to describe it other than say the Saxons had
the advantage of being uphill from the Normans, and after
an unsuccessful charge the Normans retreated. The Saxons
went chasing after them, giving up their good elevated
position, and William, noting this, rallied his men who turned about and destroyed the enemy forces. Harold had been

pierced in the eye by an arrow aimed skyward dropping on the up-looking King Harold.

The present abbey was the abbot's lodging, but is now a girl's school. Langton House is the museum containing relics from the Neolithic Age to the contemporary, dealing with Sussex history.

Hastings and the adjoining St. Leonards, to its west, are sea-bathing resorts with mild winter climate. The ruined castle on the hill up from the sea-front provides a scenic view. Hastings was one of the original Cinque Forts (first named by Edward the Confessor and later granted a charter by Edward I), the others were Romney, Hythe, Dover, and Sandwich—their main duty being to provide maritime defense of the southern coast of England. Hasting's harbour has vanished almost completely by the encroaching sea. There was little to interest me here other than the scanty ruins of the castle which was founded by William the Conqueror. It commands a view of Eastbourne and Beachy Head to the west.

I never like to leave a town or village without visiting at least one church. That's where you find your melodrama, generally. And sure enough, here at All Saints, a pretty Perpendicular church, was a plaque saying that here Titus Oates was baptized in 1660 and was for a short time curate under his father (who was rector from 1660 till 1690). Oates was the notorious English conspirator who, in 1678, forged documents which professed to reveal a scheme to murder Charles II. It was called the Papist Plot. Eventually the accusations were dropped, but in the long run Oates was tried for perjury, convicted, sentenced to imprisonment and whipping. When James II came to the throne Oates was pardoned and given a pension, but being obsessed with plottings he spent the rest of his life concocting one kind or another.

Winchelsea lies on a knoll. The original town was destroyed by the encroachments of the sea, so the town was refounded by Edward I at the end of the thirteenth century. John Wesley was supposed to have preached his last open-air sermon under an elm tree on the west side of the lovely church here. . . many years later, though.

Then reaching Rye we did the tourist thing and went to the Mermaid Inn, dating from the sixteenth century.

The summers are crowded with the golf lovers who frequent the links here. In the old church we saw a little girl take her newly purchased music box from its wrapping. Her English nanny was consumed with one of the ancient tombs and didn't see her young charge winding up the mechanism . . . and in the next moment strains of 'Fur Elise' broke the reverential silence. Beethoven had never before had such a shushing-up. After the church visit we went to the Ypres (pronounced 'wipers') Towers, the local

museum, built in the thirteenth century. Looking at the exhibits of Cinque Ports, ships and local pottery I suddenly heard the nagging, insistent theme of 'Fur Elise' . . . I wasn't the only one who couldn't get it out of her head; it was coming from the puckered lips of the softly whistling nun, who had also heard the errant music box in the sanctuary.

Badding Tower survived a burning in 1377, but was abandoned a hundred years later and sold to a John Ypres, from whom the building got its name. It had been an old

On reaching Rye we did the tourist thing and went to Mermaid Inn, a house of the late fifteen hundreds.

203

town fort and had served for many purposes including a prison for three years. The building is square with three round towers and a curious detached tower. The garden below is terraced and has a view over the river.

Our return to the car took us back to Mermaid Street, the best known thoroughfare. We were amused by the sign on a house across from the 'Mermaid Inn' that read 'The House Opposite'. The occupants had become so tired of visitors inquiring about the location of the popular Inn that they just hung a placard that gave their old door knocker a rest.

About a mile from the town is old Camber Castle, built in Henry VIII's Hythe, another of the Cinque Ports. During the Napoleonic Wars the English feared an attack by Bonaparte, so they constructed the Royal Military Canal. Gardens are planted about it now, and it's the scene of the summer Water Festival. The object of our search here was to find Saltwood Castle. It was built in 1160 — but was much older than that. On a cold winter day four knights held a rendezvous at the castle. Their names were Fitzurze, de Bret, de Moreville and de Tracy . . . and they mounted their horses and rode off to Canterbury where they found Thomas Becket, the Archbishop of Canterbury, awaiting them. He had anticipated his own martyrdom and didn't wince or try to hide as the armed four entered the cathedral to murder him, each knight thinking he was serving his king who was overheard muttering, "Who will rid me of this wretched bishop!"

The castle at Saltwood was granted to the Archbishop of Canterbury by King John, son of Henry II, later to be presented to Henry VIII by Cranmer, restored in Victorian times and now a private house. It is opened to visitors at scheduled periods during the summer.

Dover! . . . or Dubrae, as the Romans called her . . . who hasn't heard that name . . . a land atop a deep green water banked by sheer rock carved out of the stone many thousands of years ago. When the North Sea first began to eat through the western end of the Continent of Europe, it cut a path so deep that it finally broke into the land continuity and formed a new place of its own . . . Then England was born.

More visitors to England have set their feet first on

One mile north of Hythe (one of the cinque ports) is Saltwood Castle where the murderers of Becket met for their journey to Canterbury. At Canterbury they hacked the poor man to death.

land at Dover than at any other port since Roman times, being only twenty miles across the Channel to France. Perhaps the most interesting thing we saw was the Castle with its *Pharos*—the oldest standing lighthouse in England (a left-over of a Roman fortress); the Church of St. Mary de Castro built of Roman bricks and restored by the Saxons; the *Keep*, built by Henry II in the twelfth century; Harold's Well, about three hundred feet deep, older than the Castle; and the gun emplacements set up during Napoleon's wars.

Dover has played a major role in England's history since the Romans arrived before the first century A.D. It has survived many invasion threats and the more modern bombardments of two aerial wars.

Walmer Castle is up the coast a mile or so to the east. Both Walmer and Deal Castles can be visited in an hour's time. Walmer was the residence of the Lord Warden of the five Cinque Ports. Henry VIII built it against the possibility of the French invading England. It wasn't needed until 1941; at that time Churchill refused to live there, as he feared it would be a more desired target for the enemy. The

205

former Prime Minister of Australia, Sir Roland Menzies, resides there when he comes to Great Britian on business. Many famous people have been guests or residents: Lord Wellington, Pitt, Queen Victoria and Prince Albert. With all the modifications to the Castle it seems more like a manor house. About a mile to the north is Deal, a popular resort town with little interest to the traveller other than its castle. There are some old alleyways that lead off from the Promenade where smugglers used to hang out. Deal Castle, built in the 1530s, is a unique-looking construc-

Saltwood Castle.

tion . . . round and scalloped, containing one hundred and forty-five gun embrasures. The only time it has seen action was during the Civil Wars. It had belonged to the Royalists but after several weeks' siege it fell to the Parliamentarians. There is a famous Lifeboat Station on display. The distress-calls that the Walmer lifeboatmen have responded to are over two thousand. About five miles offshore is an island that once belonged to King Harold II's father. But the most fascinating of all is a plaque marking the spot where Julius Caesar landed in 55 B.C. near the lifeboat station.

206

We must return to our hotel, as it is very late, but tomorrow we can take a straight road from Gatwick to Sandwich, a picturesque old town that was once one of the most important naval bases in England. Richborough Castle—what remains of it—was Roman. The museum of the Anglo-Saxon period is in a room of the Guildhall, a fifteen-hundred building. I liked the over-hanging upper stories of the houses that seem to be typical of the town. St. Clement's is a fine parish church, dating from the Norman period, but St. Peter's dominates the center of town, whereas the Church of St. Mary the Virgin (also Norman), which is rarely used is very interesting. Golfers will be attracted to the popular golf courses; Royal St. George is one of the finest in England; others may prefer Prince's or the Royal Cinque Ports Links.

After Sandwich's port had silted up, Ramsgate became important. It appears that all George IV ever had to do to popularize a place was to visit it and like it . . . then Victorian-styled buildings sprang up everywhere. In 449 A.D. the lengendary Anglo-Saxon leaders Horsa and Hengist landed at Ebbsfleet a short distance out in Pegwell Bay about a mile west of Ramsgate. A Viking longship replica commerates the historical event. In a more modern vein is the Ramsgate Hoverport; from here the Channel can be crossed in forty minutes to Calais.

In 597 A.D. St. Augustine sailed to England with a group of monks to bring Christianity to the Anglo-Saxons in the Island. He landed a short distance from the Hoverport. In St. George's parish church there are stained-glass windows honouring the Dunkirk evacuation.

Three Days in London

The next day we would be in London—and this is how we saw it. I knew all the Kings and Queens since the reign of Edward the Confessor—had memorized them in anticipation of a some-day trip. 'Someday' had finally arrived. This was before Gatwick was used as a tourist's airport, so we hired a car at Heathrow Terminal (soon to get rid of it after a day, since Earl's Court was so accessible to the buses and underground). In fact, when Heathrow was selected as the London Airport men began to dig things up, and calling for an archaeologist, they discovered a Roman temple and village dating back to 500 B.C. The contents of some of the huts are now residing in the British Museum. I immediately became thrilled with all the antiquity.

Now, the first settlement of London was founded very soon after the invasion of Claudius, but was destroyed by Boudicca Queen of the Britons in A.D. 61. It had been on the north side of the river, so there must have been an existing bridge across the Thames. Some of the latest Roman finds came to light about ninety-five years ago indicating the remote worship of Mithraic sculptures, and later on one of Isis.

Upon arising the next morning and getting breakfast we departed to see the 'City of London'. The 'City' contains about a square mile of area which was for a long time the walled-in original London. It excludes the West End where the wonderful landmarks are of Buckingham Palace, Houses of Parliament, etc. But the exciting hub-bub exists in the old 'City'.

We take the underground to Monument Station, and on surfacing from the "Fish Street Hill" exit we are confronting the great fluted column by Christopher Wren. This was built to the memory of the horrible fire of London—the fire of 1666 that destroyed Old St. Paul's Cathedral, the London Bridge, all of Cheapside, Cripplegate—and thirteen thousand houses flattened into ashes. It had started burning on a September Sunday morning and roared on furiously until Friday. And what a miracle: not a life was lost.

I could close my eyes and see the walled city of the Middle Ages: the noise of the waggon wheels rumbling over the cobblestones was deafening; maids were crying 'cherries—like ruby lips'; coalmen, milkmen, mousetrap men and scissors grinders all screaming their wares.

My fantasy was exploded by my husband suggesting a climb to the top of the monument—which is, incidentally, the tallest free-standing column in the world. I went of course . . . and that taught me not to venture up the Tower

This great fluted column by Christopher Wren was built to the memory of the horrible fire of 1666 that destroyed Old St. Paul's Cathedral, the London Bridge, all of Cheapside, Cripplegate and thirteen thousand houses. But what a miracle — not a life was lost!

of Pisa at a later date; *leaning* would have been worse than *perpendicular!*

We entered the 'city' at the point of the world's greatest concentration of financial and commercial activity—and yet (here is what is so fascinating about London) only around the block or so is the peace and tranquility of heaven within the walls of an ancient little church. It was noontime and a Mozart recital was in progress. Businessmen and shoppers took out their cold lunches, helped themselves to the free coffee, and slid into a pew. We followed suit—I even had two rolls and a sausage left from breakfast. Off came my shoes—not to come on again, as a blister had popped on the left heel. At the last cadence of the Requiem all filed out of the sanctuary of All Hallows Barking by the Tower except us. The verger consented to take us to the crypt of the older part of the seventh century section where excavations were found from the Roman times. All Hallows was not burned in the Fire of 1666, but was bombed in the Second World War and rebuilt by Lord Mottistone in 1957. It had been saved earlier by William Penn, naval commander, who had the initiative to make a fire-break to check the flames from spreading.

We skipped the fishmarket in Fish Street—the aroma indicated its proximity. We would head for the Tower which is within walking distance of All Hallows, me barefooted due to the sores on my rubbed heels. Time at the Tower would consume the rest of the afternoon. Strictly speaking, the Tower of London and its bridge are not in the 'city', but are so close and so typically the spirit of Medieval Ages that we will visit them now. Some historians say there was a palace built for Julius Caesar here on the site almost a thousand years before William the Conqueror erected the White Palace—or Tower—as a fortress. From here he controlled all England. In the thirteenth century the two outer walls were added. King John used it during his reign to protect himself against his rebellious barons. The Tower is famous for many things: the Beefeaters (Yeomen Wardens) in their resplendent uniforms; the Crown Jewels; its 'Bloody Tower'; the graffito scratched on the inside walls by doomed prisoners; the story of the two murdered Princes (sons of King Edward IV); the jail-keep of a future great queen; and the long list of illustrious heads that rolled on Tower Hill outside the Palace with their bodies thrown in unhallowed ground. Some that died on the block on its grounds were Sir Walter Raleigh, Archbishop Laud, Sir Thomas More, Lady Jane Grey and her husband, Anne Boleyn, Catherine Howard, and many others.

The tower has four chapels, but the oldest is St. John's, built in 1080. It was where the Knights of the Bath spent all night before being dubbed. When Knights ceased to be, the chapel fell into disuse and became a storage room

until Prince Albert, consort to Victoria, restored it. In the afternoons the sunlight seems to glow right through the ancient stone—looking like transluscent or frosted glass.

The Great Hall is dedicated to Armour, most of which was made by German and Flemish armourers in the early 1500's. On the walls hang different types of weaponry; shown are the suits of Henry VIII, Elizabeth I, Prince Edward VI, and Robert Dudley (Earl of Leicester).

The Jewel Tower seems to be the main attraction for American tourists. In 1066 Edward the Confessor placed his robes and crown in Westminister Abbey, but, by the time of Charles I, what had survived of the Crowned Jewels was destroyed by Oliver Cromwell and his Parliament. Possibly a few pieces of the frame of St. Edward's crown and some baubles were saved. All was moved to the Tower. Henry VII's crown is there, reworked from a few left-overs of the old Imperial Crown. After the Restoration of the Monarchy it was re-set with precious and semi-precious stones, and the purple miniver-trimmed Cap of Estate was

The Tower of London is famous for many splendors, but also tragedies; the saddest is the tiny square outside the building where many illustrious heads fell at the chopping block, some of which were Sir Walter Raleigh, Archbishop Laud, Sir Thomas More, Lady Jane Grey and her husband, Anne Boleyn, Catherine Howard and others.

211

re-lined. It is now used for all British Coronations of their sovereigns.

As we left the Tower we bade farewell to the black ravens that stood vigil through the ages. And may they perch on forever, as it's told that as long as they remain England will be invincible.

The underground back to Earl's Court was balm to my aching feet. Tomorrow those pretty red shoes stay in the luggage—sandals would have to do for St. Paul's Cathedral. The first Cathedral was built by Augustine in 610 and burned to ashes in 961. A replacement was completed in 1087, but, alas, it too burned to the ground when a fire swept through the city of London. A third building was started immediately and on such a large scale that, had it been finished, would have been the most enormous ecclesiastical structure in the world. In the 230 years that it took in building, it slowly grew to a height of over five hundred feet. Then it was again utterly destroyed by the Great Fire of 1666.

When you enter by the south door of St. Paul's look above your head—few ever do—there is a sculptured phoenix arising from the flames. Underneath is the word "Resurgam" (I shall rise again). What could be more appropriate than this for the fourth one to be erected!

Sir Christopher Wren was selected to construct the Cathedral. The previous one had been so tremendous that eight years was required to clear away old debris before the new one could be started. A completely different style was used by the architect, as a new spirit was reawakening—a potpourri of the ancient cultures combined to a pleasing effect. It was built in the form of a cross; the great dome which rises at the intersection of the nave and transept stands out today high above the skyline, making a visible landmark for miles around. It was only thirty-five years in its structuring. Wren died before his interior plans for decoration were carried out, so the mosaic lining incrusted with gold and precious stones was never added.

The remains of Sir Christopher Wren repose at the extreme east of the south aisle. . . the only 'great' that hasn't a monument honouring him . . . merely a line, "Reader, if you seek of monument, look about you." Statues are plentiful there—some of England's famous art-

213

ists, Lord Nelson, the Duke of Wellington, John Donne in his morbid shroud and others. Donne was carved by Nicholas Stone just before the Fire and brought here from the previous St. Paul's as the only object salvaged. The pomp and circumstance may be in Westminister— crowning of Kings and Queens and solemn laying of them to rest—but St. Paul's reflects the hub of life and activity and the triumphs of the British. After the fire-gutting of London, fifty-three churches had to be rebuilt and this one

The previous St. Paul's Cathedral was so large that it took eight years to clear its debris. The present one was begun by Sir Christopher Wren in 1673.

The exterior of St. Paul's Cathedral.

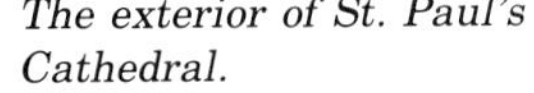

215

constituted most of Wren's lifework. It is interesting as you visit each to note that no two steeples are alike. All over England the influence of the 'dome' can be seen, for example: Castle Howard, Chiswick House, the Pantheon at Stourhead, Radcliffe Camera at Oxford University, Ickworth House, the squared domes at Osterley Park House, twin domes of the Royal Naval College and many more.

The afternoon will be spent in Smithfield. The best way to get there from St. Paul's is on foot. Cut through Paternos Square to Newgate Street then veer slighty west to Giltspur Street and you are in West Smithfield. You passed St. Bartholomew's Hospital on the right, close to the Church of St. Bartholomew the Great. In this district there are no new streets, but it abounds in old enclosures, alleyways and lanes like Long Lane and Duck Lane. It was half a century after the Norman Conquest before this parcel of land was built on; it was really slightly outside of the 'city', so there was no jurisprudence over the area. In 1123 a Priory was founded by Rahere, a courtier and jester of Henry I. He vowed while on a crusade to Rome, where he became very ill, that if he could return home in healed condition he would build a church and hospital in thanksgiving. This he did. His beautifully carved tomb lies on the north side between two columns near the beginning of the apse. Another interesting feature is an oriel window in the south wall of the choir. This was added by Prior Bolton in 1520. It was said he sat inside looking over the congregation while the offering plate was passed. Beneath the window is a curious rebus—the signature of the Prior—a crossbow bolt transfixing a tun or cask, meaning 'Bolt-in-ton'.

We climbed up to the bell-tower and watched the skilled pullers ring the bells, at which witnessing we realized what artistry it demanded.

Leaving the Church of St. Bartholomew the Great my eyes fell on these words; "This spiritual house, Almighty God shall inhabit, and hallow it, and glorify it, and His eyes shall be opened, and His ears intending on this house night and day, that the asker in it shall receive, the seeker shall find, and the ringer or knocker shall enter."

And now we are in Smithfield Square. When Mary

At Smithfield there is the old priory of St. Bartholomew the Great, built by the jester of Henry I, Rahere, who vowed while on a Crusade to Rome that if he could return to England healed of his illness he would build a house for God.

Tudor became queen she felt she had much of her father's sin to atone for and undo. As part of her 'divinely-inspired' plan she must reduce all England to Catholic orthodoxy. Smithfield became a bonfire of the first Protestant martyrs . . . and the odor of that deed still hovers over her memory.

Heading on for the Strand we visit the Royal Courts of Justice. I recall Byron's lines on viewing this site looking down Fleet Street curving toward Ludgate Hill:

217

"A wilderness of steeples peeping
On tiptoe through their sea-coal canopy;
A huge, dun cupola, looking like a foolscap crown
On a fool's head — and there is London Town!"

The thin spire is best seen long before reaching it, rising above the hipped-roof. It is designed in Gothic style and has a projecting clock hanging over the Strand side. It was built by the "ream of Augustus Pugin and Sir Charles Barry" between the years 1874-82. There is another tower on Carey Street in the back of the building, but here the style changes to the Victorian — exposed brick with stripes or bands as decoration. At this point the Old City begins to converge with the West End. . . Westminister. Here we'll take a taxi to Piccadilly Circus and from there the underground to our hotel.

It will consume most of the next day covering the area around Fleet Street. There will be Gray's Inn, Lincoln's Inn, and Temple Church, then Middle Temple, Inner Temple, and Dr. Johnson's House. We alighted from our vehicle on Fleet Street, near where the Strand ends. Once the Fleet Brook ran down the road, but was now confined in a sewer. They said it flowed with ink, being the center of the newspaper and printing life of London. This was where we left the Courts of Justice yesterday — not far from the Inn's Court, made up of the four great Inns of Court which control largely the practice and govern of the barristers of Wales and England. We looked inside of Middle Temple to see where famous men had called its rooms home: Thackeray, Dr. Samuel Johnson, and Charles Lamb. In Part One of the play *Henry VI*, Shakespeare makes the rose garden here the setting of an incident that started the Wars of Roses which was the dispute between the two houses . . . the White Rose of the Yorks and the Red Rose of the Lancasters.

Gray's Inn dates from 1370, but is vastly restored. For fifty years Sir Francis Bacon, the essayist, lived here. In the fifteen hundreds plays were given in the Hall. Lincoln's Inn has been in existence since 1422. It contains the largest law library in England and may be visited on application. Such greats as John Donne, Sir Thomas More, Gladstone,

Facing the Royal Courts of Justice on the Strand.

218

GENTLEMEN

Disraeli and William Penn had worked here. We had brought our lunch and joined the other visitors and students on the smooth green lawn and watched the friendly mingling between black-robed faculty members and scholars.

The Middle Temple has been the home of many famous people, some of which were Charles Lamb, Dr. Johnson, Thackeray and Shakespeare.

Not far away is Temple Church — this I had anticipated more than any of the ancient relics of London. There was once a bar—or gate—that spanned Fleet Street called the Temple Bar. It has now disappeared, but the church still remains. It is the largest and most important of the four existing round churches in the world, and is the finest monument in England to the Knight's Templar. The Knights were the guardians of the Holy Sepulchre in Jerusalem, and protected the roads that the pilgrims travelled to get there. The interior columns are built in Purbeck marble and date from the eleven hundreds. The full title of the order was Poor Knights of Christ and the Temple of Solomon. They took vows of chastity, obedience, and poverty. Offenses that might expel a member included desertion to the Saracens, heresy, losing the gonfalon (a flag which hung from a frame), murdering a Christian, and failing to account for any property of the order in his possession.

After the next two hundred years something went wrong. The Templars saw an opportunity to become extremely rich; they were the international bankers of their day. Soon kings envied their thriving resources. And just how true, nobody has been able to prove beyond a doubt—charges were made of human sacrifices and witchcraft, to which, after imprisonment and hideous torture, plus the old trick of each one being told that his fellows had already confessed, each surrendered himself.

The London Temple was dissolved, but the church remains and houses students of the common law. We entered the large scantily furnished room and I immediately found the object of my quest: the incumbent figure of William Marshall entombed in the center of the room. He was sculptured in his full armour regalia. William Marshall was so called because he was the marshall of England . . . and Earl of Pembroke, also the greatest fighting man of that age, not excluding Richard Coeur de Lion, with the battle-ax. His character and principles were of the highest standard. When Richard I died there was a struggle over the inheritance, as Coeur de Lion never stayed home long enough to provide an heir, much to the grief of the quiet lovely Berengaria of Navarre. Young Arthur of Brittany was living in France—many liked him and thought he had a more rightful claim, but William Marshall shook his grizzled old head in refusal; he prevailed on the powers to take John (in spite of his meaness) over Arthur. John later blinded Arthur to ensure his hold on the throne, since no blind man could be King of England.

John was a pox on the English people (even if his over-bearance did bring something good . . . the writing of Magna Charta demanding the king's signature . . .) but William Marshall stuck it out with the would-be despot, helping him in many scrapes with the French King. When the wicked English King was dying he trusted only one man; he dictated a statement to William that he was to be the guardian of his son and heir, who became King Henry III.

We leave the Round Temple on this note—that it's better to be well-thought-of for centuries than to be wealthy and king for a lifetime.

It's still too soon for 'high tea', so while we are in the neighborhood we will walk about three blocks west on Fleet Street until Gough Square appears—one block north of Fleet—you can't miss it because someone is always around with city maps. Here is the home of Dr. Johnson, a late seventeenth-century house. It contains many mementos of

222

the great man. He was born in Lichfield, 1709 . . . and at
an early age showed a precocity that ripened into what
made him the literary dictator in the last half of his century. He was somewhat self-educated through his voracious
study of the Latin classics, even amazing the faculty at Oxford University. He tried his hand at teaching, but his
idiosyncrasies caused him to lose his post. On moving to
London he started to hack-write. Writing, at this time, was
not a very lucrative livelihood. But in 1747 some
booksellers in London got together with the idea of
publishing a dictionary of the English language. Upon being approached Johnson accepted. The poor fellow "turned
off" quite a few who could have made monetary contributions had he not been so atrociously bad mannered. It was
finally finished in 1755. While he worked on his for-
midable volume he also contributed some essays and articles called *The Rambler.*

Finally, after many incidents of literary fiascoes, he
went to debtors prison. By 1762, though, a Tory leader took
a fancy to his writings and saved him from total starvation

*Dr. Johnson's house is
across the street from the
Cheshire Cheese. Its site
is one block north of Fleet
Street.*

. . . and not only that, he became a pivot in an influential literary group of men who dubbed themselves "Johnson's Circle". But it was Boswell who made him remembered for what he had accomplished—and not so much Johnson's writings themselves.

I examined a few of his definitions that are priceless for their humour and cutting edge:

> Oats: a grain which in England is generally given to horses, but in Scotland supports the people.
> Willow: a tree worn by forlorn lovers.
> Excise: a hateful tax levied on commodities, and adjudged, not by common judges of properties but wretches hired by those to whom excise is paid.
> Transpire: to escape from secrecy to notice, a sense lately innovated from France without necessity.

I don't remember where we dropped in for tea, but with the dainties that came along on the teacart we could hold out without dinner until after the play. This was a Saturday so there would be a five o'clock performance at The Ambassadors Theatre of Agatha Christie's *The Mousetrap.*

This production is one of her fourteen plays, but her eightieth book was published on her eightieth birthday, which was in 1970. She was acclaimed the most widely read British writer in the world with Shakespeare coming in a poor second. She is lovingly called "The Duchess of Death", and like her literary equal, Daphne du Maurier, she hated pomp. When *Mousetrap* opened November 25th, 1952, Sir Winston Churchill was Prime Minister, Harry S. Truman was President of U.S.A. and Stalin was Head of Russia. If all the people who have seen her plays at The Ambassador formed a queue it would reach the Highlands of Scotland—almost three million people.

After the play we took a taxi back toward Earl's Court Road. The driver recommended a cozy restaurant close by our hotel. It was *The Secret Place.* Not much to look at (that accounted, I suppose, for it's privacy) . . . a peek inside was a different matter. The decor was simple, but most unusual: the tables were old butcher blocks scrubbed almost white (I remembered when I was a child and spent the summers with my farming grandparents in

224

Burnt Corn, Alabama—buckets of sand were emptied on the kitchen floor and it was my brother's job to scrub the pine boards until they shone like satin wood. What delicious nostalgia!—but back to 243 Old Brompton Road). We were welcomed in front of a roaring fire, for the night was cool and the old thick walls had not retained much warmth from the cloudy day. The copper pots gleamed against the dead-white walls along with other bits of past centuries—old objets d'art. We felt so festive that we braved the wildest items on the menu—something surely that wouldn't have been served in my grandparent's kitchen: A Morgan Furze wine followed by Avocat creme et caviar, soupeaux moules, truit aux bananes and souffle. Try our culinary adventure once—I bet you would like it. Tomorrow we will 'do' the Victoria Embankment that makes a parkway of the bank of the Thames River.

The next day was a nice one for exploring—a quiet Sunday with very little activity astir. Taking a public conveyance we headed for Charing Cross; incidentally, very few may realize this landmark's significance. This junction was the last stage of Queen Eleanor of Castile's funeral progress before entering Westminister Abbey for burial in 1290. Edward I grieved so deeply for his beloved queen that he erected beautifully adorned crosses at each processional stopping place—from Harby, where she died, to London. Others were at Lincoln, Grantham, Stamford, Geddington, Stony Stratford, Woborn, St. Albans and Waltham (just north of London).

From Charing Cross we walked down Northumberland until we reached the Victoria Embankment which is a stretch of parkway between Blackfriars and Westminister Bridge of a mile in length. Some of the lands that were reclaimed from the Thames River, used for laying in sewer lines, needed to be beautified. In 1862 many memorials were placed there, some very attractive. Near the Waterloo Bridge at Lancaster Place stands the imposing building called Somerset House. It is entered on the Strand side and backs up to the Embankment with a lovely frontage.

In 1547 the young King Edward VI, son of Jane Seymour and Henry VIII, was orphaned. The Duke of Somerset, protector of the nine year old sovereign, decided to build himself a palace, so he took stone from St. Mary-le-Strand to lay the foundation. It never got finished before he was executed five years later. During Queen Mary's reign Elizabeth I lived there—as did the queens of James I, Charles I and II. In 1776 another building was erected over the site and it is used for administrative offices. Wills are stored here, some date from the thirteen hundreds; if you wish to see Van Dyck's, Florence Nightingale's, Dickens', Shakespeare's—then go there. That is where we went to look for the dispersing of the Isaac M. Singer fortune (the inventor of the Singer sewing machine—not that we looked for anything left over, but his being a relative of Dick's made a good excuse to see Somerset House). A big-to-do was made of opening and closing filing drawers and cabinets, and finally being directed to Coutt's Bank. We *did* find out that most of the fortune went to his son, Paris, and then to Isadora Duncan, famous barefoot dancer. But, since she and their small son both died (in separate auto accidents) we went on from there and found that a distant relative lived in opulence in Grovesner Square on 'ample

crumbs' left from the fortune. That gave us a sense of 'sorta' belonging there—one of the poor kin, so to speak.

Back to the Strand at Lancaster Place, a little searching will reward you with the glorious Savoy Chapel wedged in behind the Savoy Hotel and the Savoy Theatre. In 1245 this was built and became property later of John of Gaunt, the Duke of Lancaster, until it burned during a tax rebellion (led by Wat Tyler in 1381). A hundred years later it was rebuilt by Henry VII, about the same time that Sir Thomas Malory's *Morte Darthur* was printed on Caxton's new presses—hence the naming of Henry VII's first son, Prince Arthur. The Chapel we see here was remodeled by Queen Victoria. Geoffrey Chaucer had married at its altar in the late thirteen hundreds and presented the picture hanging above it to the sanctuary.

Returning to the Embankment and going west we see the famous Boudicca monument. Here is a wonderful subject for a photo shot with Big Ben in the background. Boudicca was queen of the Britons in 61 A.D. It was she who drove the Romans out of London. Not far away is Cleopatra's Needle in pink granite standing 88 feet tall. It was presented to Great Britain in 1819 by the Viceroy of Egypt Mohammed Ali. The monolith was first set up in Heliopolis in the fourteen hundreds. There are two others existing: one in Central Park (New York City) and the other at Place de la Concorde in Paris. The hieroglyphics are supposed to tell the history of Thutmose III and Rameses II. The one in London was placed on the Embankment in 1878.

Turning eastward we find close to the Waterloo Bridge, the *S.S. Discovery*, famous ship,—now used as a recruiting vessel—and three training ships, *President, Chrysanthemum*, and the *Wellington*.

The first Waterloo Bridge was built in 1817 as part of a road system which spanned the Thames. A hundred and six years later its 70,000 tons was demolished and a new one erected by Sir G. Gilbert Scott, and as lovely as you would expect from Scott's drawing board. It was a thing of beauty. The best views of the river can be seen from it. We crossed and looked back to the north at Somerset House and its watergate. If you continue on this road you arrive at the Elephant and Castle—which landmark, had

The S. S. Discovery, a famous ship, is moored on the Thames embankment close to the Waterloo Bridge.

The Houses of Parliament.

given us so much trouble two years ago due to its five-way intersection.

We were to visit the Royal Festival Hall on the south bank of the river, but it wasn't open, so we took the Riverside Walk and went west toward the London County Hall situated next to the south end of the Westminster Bridge. This leads to the Houses of Parliament. There stands mighty old Big Ben. The first bridge to span the Thames was the Roman London Bridge—Westminster was next, built in the mid-seventeen hundreds. This one lasted about sixty years and was replaced by the present one. Close by is the statue of Boudicca that we saw earlier. At the Westminster pier a pleasure boat can be taken down the river to Greenwich—also up river to Hampton Court. Either trip will consume most of a day—but how delightful! The afternoon would be spent at Westminster Abbey and that would complete our day.

I knew most of the history of this splendid old edifice . . . that its conception began in Edward the Confessor's time, although there are intimations of a previous

228

house of worship on the site. A legend says there was a monastery here in the six hundreds during Saxon days. The *Morte Darthur* of Mallory tells of King Arthur holding a tournament close by—that Elaine was buried in a field next to the monastery. But more of substance is a tomb in the present abbey of King Sebert (died 616) that was erected in 1308 by the monks.

Facts are, though, that Edward the Confessor did build Westminster on what then was a little island called Thorney Island, which was later cleared and drained into what we see today. He had a palace constructed, almost joining it, to watch the progress of the Abbey. Whether he did this intentionally to strengthen the bond between Church and State is unknown, but for the next five centuries the palace at Westminster became the King's reigning domain and during the period from 1376 to 1547 eight of the kings and queens were buried in the Abbey next door.

After the mid-sixteen hundreds the Palace became the Houses of Parliament. Of the construction of Edward the Confessor's nothing is left, as it was demolished and Henry III rebuilt it two hundred years later, placing the tomb of the Confessor in its original location. By then he was referred to as St. Edward. King Henry impoverished himself to provide for the memory of the founder by magnificent ornaments for the shrine. It is considered the most sacred spot in the Abbey, but has been despoiled twice and will never regain the glory of its original state. Some stones were replaced during Queen Mary's reign, and if you look carefully at the east end you can see the substitutes for yourself. But back to earlier days.

Christmas Day 1065 was planned for the consecration of the Abbey, however, the king was ill so it was postponed until the 28th . . . on January 5th the king died. Harold succeeded him, though there is no confirmed evidence of his coronation here. But in this same awful year a foreigner, the Duke of Normandy, William the Conqueror, fought Harold in battle. Harold died. William was to be crowned at the Abbey. Just as the ceremony started, a terrible babbling of Saxon and Norman tongues filled the air—no one understanding the other's language—it raised such a threatening cacophony that the guards without the Abbey thought a riot had begun. Then someone spotted

Westminster Abbey was rebuilt by Henry III, who placed the tomb of Edward the Confessor, the original founder, in its center.

flames near the Abbey gate and a clamour of "Fire, fire" arose, and in a few seconds the entire Abbey was emptied except for William and the clergyman. So in a lonely hall the diadem was placed on the Duke's head—no triumphant music, no congratulations, no friend's voice. This was prophetic of his morbid end in France, where he had gone to oversee his estate. Quarrelling started between himself and the king of France, his overlord. William grew furious and set fire to a village in the Seine valley. The next day, riding to the area to inspect his bit of arson, his horse reared and William was thrown upon the hot ashes. He lingered very ill several weeks in pain then died unwept for. Next to be seen was the Coronation Chair.

There is so much beauty in this place that it cannot be taken in on one visit. The many elegant monuments and their magnitude almost play havoc with the wonderful architecture of the sanctuary, seeming to obliterate it. In no other place in the world has there been brought together in as small a space so much to astound the senses . . . be it art, music, sculpture, architecture. But the one particular point of interest is the function and solemnity of the object before us in the St. Edward's Chapel. The Coronation Chair was fashioned by Master Walter of Durham in 1300, during the reign of Edward I. The King designed it to contain the Stone of Scone (Scūn) which had been captured from the Scots in 1296. It was believed to be the stone upon which Jacob laid his head . . . ". . . Jacob . . . went toward Haran . . . and he took of the stones of that place, and put them for his pillow, and laid down in that place to sleep. And he dreamed, and behold a ladder set up on the earth, and the top of it reached to heaven, and behold the angels of God ascending and descending on it . . ." (King James Version). The Kings of Scotland sat upon it at their coronations. In England it has been used for every coronation service since 1296 except for that of Edward V and Edward VIII (that was because Edward V was murdered as a boy and Edward VIII rejected his inheritance).

Henry VII's Chapel is considered the most beautiful in all Christendom. It was constructed in 1503 for the king and his queen, Elizabeth of York, and is now the Chapel of the Knights of the Most Honourable Order of the Bath. The complex vaulting of its ceiling reminds one of Bath

Abbey, King's College at Cambridge, and the cloisters at Gloucester Cathedral.

Nowhere displays the history and pageantry of England in stone as does Westminster Abbey. It was not until the early part of the eighteen hundreds that the public was admitted in its sanctuary—if they entered, it was only through the permission of the Dean. But today thousands of visitors throng its nave everyday to view the resting place of all the greatest poets, writers, musicians, warriors, nobility, historians, even an actor . . . and next to him a clock-maker, Tompion. I'll write no more about this illustrious structure, but leave you to explore its wonders. Built so long ago as a House of Prayer, every visitor upon leaving its portals should at least offer up a prayer for peace on earth in our time.

This day we awoke to a nip of fall in the air. "Couldn't we walk to Hyde Park, it looks so close to Earl's Court on the map." "You *could* but you'd be too tired to see anything then." We went downstairs to breakfast and sat across from people of far away places. One could tell by their head dress; the lady opposite me wore bangles over her brow that was additionally adorned with a large scarlet spot (I dared not scrutinize the situation to determine if it were a jewel imbedded in flesh or a detachable bauble), then another next to her, with such slit eyes that they seemed to be pulled and sewn to her temples, poked furtively at her viands . . . then that turbaned figure—and what was he doing . . . putting sugar on fried eggs! Oh well, this is a continental hotel.

We caught a bus and climbed to the upper deck—the view was good. There were piles and piles of stone stacked into beautifully shaped buildings . . . and marble arches. I closed my eyes and saw the strange island of Portland, down on the south coast of Dorset, with its big empty belly of a mountain—scooped out to delight the eyes of Londoners. From there had come the great pulpit of St. Paul's Cathedral, the Wellington Arch—and so on. How the mother-quarry must miss her lovely offspring!

The sudden jolt of the bus opened my eyes at Hyde Park Corner. "Well, hello there!" It was the Wellington Arch! This was erected by a women's group to commerorate the victories of the great Duke Arthur Wellesley,

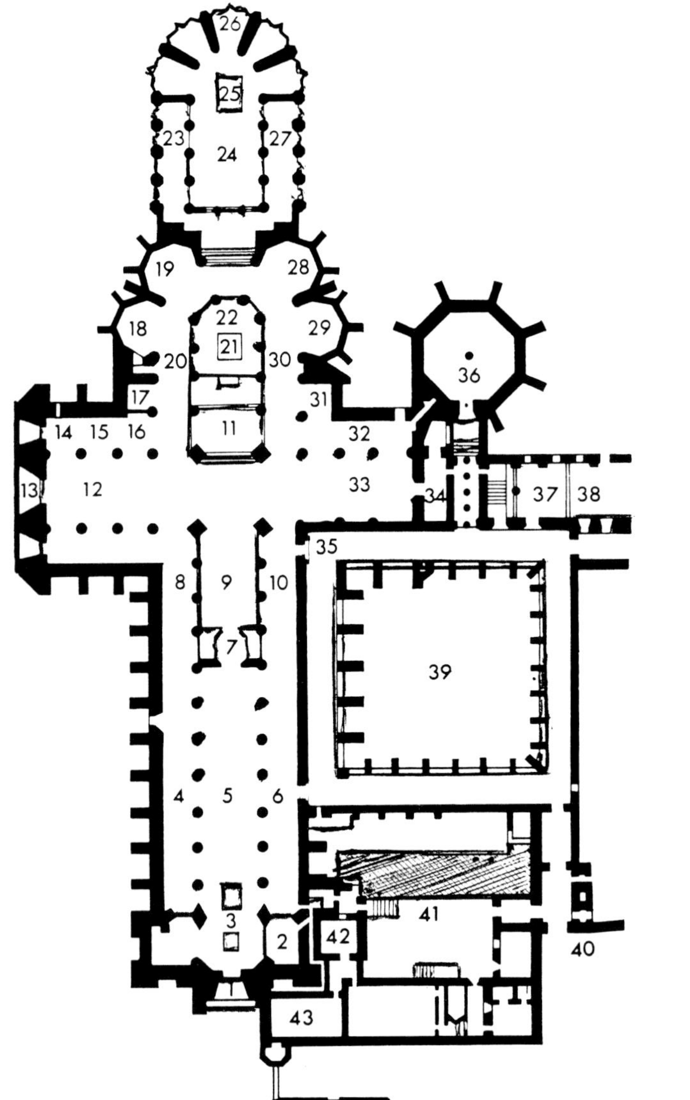

A tomb dedicated to the 'unknown soldier' is in the floor near the entrance of Westminster Abbey.

hero of Waterloo, where Napoleon made his feeble stand. Through the archway is Rotten Row—a mile-long track used for horse-back riding by ladies in their fancy chic habits and an occasional dandy in his scarlet pinks.

The Manor of Hyde had been given to Geoffrey de Manderville, but when he died it went to the Church. In 1536 Henry VIII had confiscated this area from Westminster Abbey and turned it into his private deer park. Charles I, a hundred years later, opened it to the public. It was also used as a dueling ground.

A very short walk took us to the Serpentine Lake. It

held interest for me—as it was here that Shelley's first wife, Harriet Westbrook, committed suicide after her 'bad boy' husband had left her for the libertine Mary Godwin, whose father and Shelley held many views on atheism and the 'tyranny of the institution of marriage' in common. The tragedy in Hyde Park, 1816, did affect Shelley to a degree that we can credit him at least for a sadness about the affair . . . even if it was just momentary.

Close to the west end of the lake is the intriguing Peter Pan statue. Tiny bronze squirrels, chipmunks, and rabbits scamper about the pedestal. A third of a mile farther we find Kinsington Palace and the Sunken Gardens. This lovely palace had been the country home of the Earl of Nottingham in the mid-sixteen hundreds, but was acquired by William III who commissioned Sir Christopher Wren to remodel the house. At the same time he turned an adjoining twenty-six acres into a formal garden, which was enlarged and elaborated upon by Queen Anne, who followed his reign, and later additions were by Queen Caroline.

The interior of the palace contains carved panels by Gringling Gibbons, flower and fruit designs festooning the archways, and profussions of richly painted walls and ceilings.

It was early afternoon by now and we wanted to see the Albert Memorial . . . long considered the ugliest monument in existence. But no more, The Victorian masterpiece has come into its own and is now appreciated as a great achievement in construction and artistry. It was designed by Gilbert Scott, who had in mind the ancient ciborium style, which was a canopy covering a high altar generally supported by four columns using metal work studded with semi-precious stones and ornamented with mosiacs. It took

236

Albert Memorial.

ten years to construct the 175 ft. high memorial, being completed in 1876. It was Queen Victoria's tribute to her dead Prince Albert—and one of the most intricate works ever erected. Photograph it when the late afternoon sun is on it—even if it takes over an hour for the clouds to break, as it did for us. You will prize the results.

All this information can be found in brochures, of course, and I'm getting a bit glutted with this hurried tourist aspect of my peregrinations. I want to go back to Cornwall in England's extreme west . . . where the shore is not so much for commerce as for dreaming, where a man can measure himself by his ability to cope with the land's monstrous adversaries: the barreness of its central body; the roughness of its cliffs; the harshness of its winter gales; the thorn and the braccen; the lichen-covered stones of antiquity—with the everpresent sea making its sometimes-sweet music. There God is, too . . . and the uncluttered highway to His abode is easiest here for me. There is no time to return now—though a silent alarm screams out, "go back . . . go back . . ." But there is a busy world and the 'big clock' is ticking on—. I must up and face it. Tonight I will dream of Cornwall; tomorrow I will be four thousand miles away. Good night, dear Lord, and hold me in your tender protection. Thank you for permitting me to come away to England.

BACH GLUCK HANDEL MOZART HAYDN. BEETHOVEN. TALLIS. O. GIBBONS LAWES. PURCELL

239

SOVEREIGNS OF ENGLAND

673—Egfred — Ethelreda

Anglo-Saxons

827—Egbert
837—Ethelwulf
866—Ethelred I
871—Alfred the Great
901—Edward the Elder
938—Athelstan
946—Edred
959—Edgar
978—Ethelred the Unready
1016—Edmund Ironside
1016—Canute the Dane
1035—Harold I
1040—Hardicanute
1042—Edward the Confessor
1066—Harold II

Normans

1066—William the Conqueror
1087—William Rufus
1100—Henry I
1135—Stephen

Plantagenets

1154—Henry II
1189—Richard I
1199—John
1216—Henry III
1272—Edward I
1307—Edward II
1327—Edward III
1377—Richard II

240

Lancastrians

1399—Henry IV
1413—Henry V
1422—Henry VI

Yorkists

1461—Edward IV
1483—Edward V
1483—Richard III

Tudors

1485—Henry VII
1509—Henry VIII
1547—Edward VI
1553—Mary I
1558—Elizabeth I

Stuarts

1603—James I
1625—Charles I
[1649—Commonwealth]
1660—Charles II
1685—James II
1688—William III and Mary II
1694—William III
1702—Anne

Hanoverians

1714—George I
1727—George II
1760—George III
[1810—Regency]
1820—George IV
1830—William IV
1837—Victoria

House of Saxe-Coburg

1901—Edward VII

House of Windsor

1910—George V
1939—George VI
1952—Elizabeth II

THE KINGS OF ENGLAND

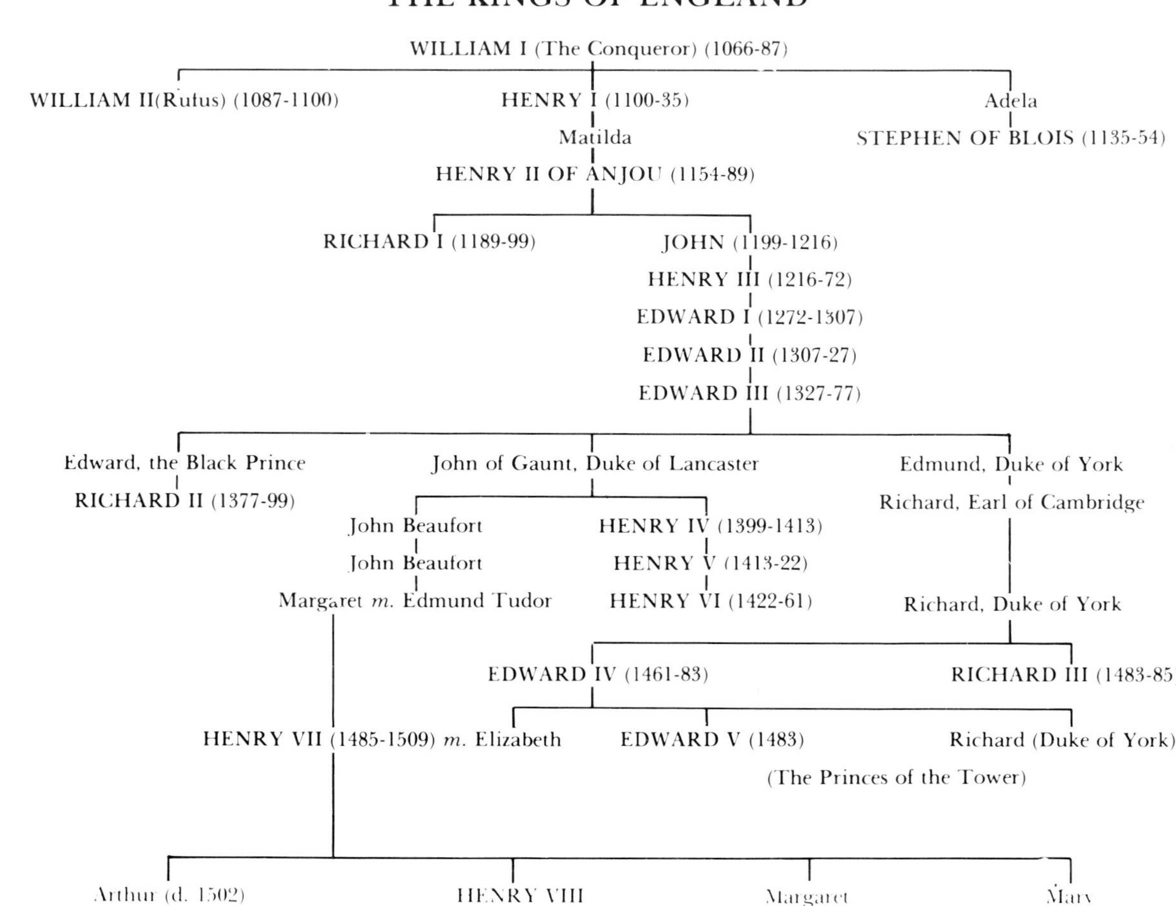

LINEAGE—HENRY VIII to 1983

HENRY VIII (Tudor)   Margaret

Catherine — M. — Jane Seymour   M.
  Mary I   Anne Boleyn   Edward VI   James IV   (STUART)
    M   Elizabeth I   James V
Philip of Spain   Mary Stuart, Queen of Scots M. Darnley

        James (Stuart VI), I of England

     Charles I m. Henrietta (Bourbon) ————————————— Elizabeth m. Frederick (Palatinate)
Charles II — James II — Mary (Stuart) m. William II   Sophia m. Ernest (HANOVER)
Anne (Queen) — Mary II m. William III (Holland)   George I Hanoverian King
                                                              George II
                                                              George III

       George IV ——— William IV ——— Edward (Duke of Kent)
                                         Victoria Queen m. Albert (Saxe-Coburg)
       Eight other children ——— Edward VII
                                   George V m. Mary Princess of Teck
             Edward (abd) ———— George VI
             Duke of Windsor

             Elizabeth II m. Philip Mountbatten — Margaret
                      Charles (Prince of Wales)

Index

SCOTLAND
Hadrian's Wall
N.
ENGLAND
LONDON
CORNWALL
G.W.